Education and Disadvantaged Children and Young People

Also available in the Education as a Humanitarian Response Series

Education as a Global Concern, Colin Brock
Education and Minorities, edited by Chris Atkin
Education and HIV/AIDS, edited by Nalini Asha Biggs
Education, Refugees and Asylum Seekers, edited by Lala Demirdjian
Education, Aid and Aid Agencies, edited by Zuki Karpinska
Education and Reconciliation, edited by Julia Paulson
Education and Natural Disasters, edited by David Smawfield
Education and Internally Displaced Persons, edited by Christine Smith and Alan Smith

Also available from Bloomsbury

Education Around the World: A Comparative Introduction, Colin Brock and Nafsika Alexiadou
Comparative and International Education: An Introduction to Theory, Method, and Practice, David Phillips and Michele Schweisfurth

Education and Disadvantaged Children and Young People

Education as a Humanitarian Response

Edited by

Mitsuko Matsumoto

BLOOMSBURY
NEW DELHI • LONDON • OXFORD • NEW YORK • SYDNEY

First published in India 2018
First published 2013

Bloomsbury Academic India
An imprint of Bloomsbury Publishing Plc
BLOOMSBURY, Bloomsbury Academic India and the
Diana logo are trademarks of Bloomsbury Publishing Plc

British Library Cataloguing-in-Publication Data
A catalogue record for this book is available from the British Library.

Library of Congress Cataloging-in-Publication Data Education and disadvantaged children and young people: education as a humanitarian response/edited by
Mitsuko Matsumoto.
pages cm. – (Education as a humanitarian response) Includes bibliographical references and index.
ISBN 978-1-4411-1796-0 (pbk.) – ISBN 978-1-4411-9799-3 (hardcover) –
ISBN 978-1-4411-9714-6 (epub) – ISBN 978-1-4411-2176-9 (pdf)
1. Children with social disabilities–Education–Case studies.
2. Youth with social disabilities–Education–Casestudies.
3. Educational equalization. I.Matsumoto, Mitsuko,1981–
LC4065.E375 2013 371.826′94–dc23
2013006860

ISBN 978 93 8800 228 8
10 9 8 7 6 5
For sale in the Indian subcontinent only

Bloomsbury Publishing India Pvt. Ltd
Second Floor, Building No. 4
DDA Complex LSC, Pocket C – 6 & 7
Vasant Kunj, New Delhi 110070
www.bloomsbury.com

Typeset by Deanta Global Publishing Services, Chennai, India
Printed and bound in India by Replika Press Pvt. Ltd.

Contents

Notes on Contributors

Natalie Brett studied Sports Management at Bournemouth University, UK; her thesis was on funding sports development and amateur sports in Canada. Following graduation, Natalie worked with KidSport Ottawa, a Canadian charity supporting disadvantaged children and youth wishing to participate in sports. She recently returned to Canada after 4 months in Botswana and prior to that she was a Capacity Support Officer for 12 months in the Falkland Islands with Commonwealth Games Canada where she worked on sports development throughout all levels of age and ability.

Margaryta Danilko is Associate Professor of Linguistics at Kirovograd State Pedagogical University, Ukraine. She also teaches at Kirovograd Regional In-Service Institute. She was an exchange scholar at Montclair State University, USA, and has worked in the field of Education for more than 24 years. She has broad research interests which include the educational response to vulnerable children, teaching for critical thinking, linguistics and English Language Teaching (ELT) methods. Her works – written in Ukrainian, English and Russian – have appeared in a variety of scholarly journal publications.

Rosalind Evans has been working with young refugees for the past 8 years. She studied at Oxford University, UK, during 2004–2009 completing an MSc in Forced Migration and a DPhil in International Development Studies, which focused on the experiences of young Bhutanese refugees growing up in long-term camps in Nepal. She is co-founder of the charity Refugee Youth Project and has worked for various organisations supporting young people and refugees in the UK, Nepal, Lebanon and Egypt.

Parker Goyer started the Coach for College program in 2008 and has since overseen the implementation of five summer programs in Vietnam, serving nearly 1500 Vietnamese middle school students. She attended Oxford University, UK, on the Rhodes Scholarship, where she received an MSc in Comparative and International Education and an MBA. She is currently in the doctoral program at the Graduate School of Education, Harvard University, USA.

Hannah Juneau studied Kinesiology at the University of Calgary, Canada, and has worked in sports at the local, national and international level in Canada for over a decade. She has focused her career on ensuring sports and physical activity is accessible to all children regardless of their socio-economic status. Hannah lives in Aylmer, Quebec and continues to volunteer for many organizations including KidSport Ottawa and her own charity, Kamatipa New Hope.

Maria Hantzopoulos is Assistant Professor of Education at Vassar College, USA, and a participating faculty member in the Urban Studies and Women's Studies Programs. She also taught and worked in New York City public schools for 13 years, served on the planning teams of several new small local high schools, and worked with a variety of established youth organizations, including ASPIRA and Seeds of Peace. Her work has appeared in a variety of scholarly journal publications and she is the co-editor, with Alia Tyner-Mullings, of *Critical Small Schools: Beyond Privatization in NYC Urban Educational Reform* (Information Age, 2012).

Colin Higgs is Professor Emeritus at Memorial University of Newfoundland, Canada. He has worked in the field of physical activity and sports for persons with a disability for more than 40 years, and has been working in the area of sports for development in Africa, the Caribbean and Central and South America since the early 1990s.

Nadiya Ivanenko is Assistant Professor of Comparative Linguistics and Vice-Dean at the Faculty of Foreign Languages at Kirovograd State Pedagogical University, Ukraine. She studied Comparative Education at Oxford University, UK, and has been working in the field of education for more than 13 years. She has published more than 25 scientific articles, textbooks and manuals. She is also a convener of the English Speaking Union in Ukraine.

Racheal Kalaba has an MA in Management of Community and Volunteer Services from Dublin City University, Ireland, and a BA in Development Studies. For the last 8 years, she has worked on development of children, youth and women at the local, national and international levels in Zambia. She focuses on promoting equality for all, with a people centered development approach. Racheal presently lives in Ndola, Zambia, and is Managing Director for PEAS Zambia, a UK NGO promoting access to education for all. She also volunteers for Kamatipa New Hope, International Rural Youth Movement, GYIN and the Department of Youth in the Copperbelt Province of Zambia.

Mitsuko Matsumoto has recently obtained a Doctor of Philosophy at the Department of Education, University of Oxford, UK. Her research examined the role of education in (the risk of) contemporary violent conflict, focusing on young people's experiences and perceptions of education in Sierra Leone. She currently collaborates with el Fundación Educación para el Empleo in Madrid, Spain. She has worked for the UN Liaison Office of Soka Gakkai International, a Buddhist association that promotes peace, culture and education. She has led 'Victory over Violence' workshops to pupils at various schools in New York city, promoting non-violent values and behaviours.

Aoife O'Higgins is a DPhil Candidate in Education at the Rees Centre at the University of Oxford, UK. Her project looks at the educational outcomes of teenagers in care. She has also completed two masters degrees, in Refugee Studies at the University of East London, UK, and in Evidence-Based Social Interventions at the University of Oxford, UK. She has worked with refugee communities since 2005, and most recently at The Children's Society as a Young Refugees' Rights Advocate in London. She has also done consultancy and capacity building work and training for a number of refugee and children's organisations as well as guest lectures on social work courses in London Universities.

Mohammad Akhtar Siddiqui has a PhD in Education and has been engaged in teaching, research and educational administration for more than three decades. He is a Professor of Education at the Faculty of Education, Jamia Millia Islamia Central University, New Delhi. Until recently, he was Chairperson of the National Council for Teacher Education, an apex body for teacher education and development under the Ministry of Human Resource Development, Government of India.

Carla Thachuk obtained a Masters focused on International Development through Sports from Memorial University of Newfoundland and University of Peace, Costa Rica. She is currently working as the Director of International Programs with Commonwealth Games Canada. Previously, she spent 3 years working with UNHCR setting up sports programs to ensure refugees throughout the world have access to safe and educational sports and play opportunities.

Zeena Zakharia is Assistant Professor of Comparative Education at the University of Massachusetts, Boston, USA. She was the Middle Eastern Studies Postdoctoral Fellow at Columbia University, USA, and Tueni Fellow at the

Carr Center for Human Rights Policy, Harvard University, USA. Her recent publications consider the interplay of language policy, collective identity, and human security in schools, during and after violent political conflict. These interests stem from over a decade of educational leadership in war-affected contexts. She is co-editor (with O. García and B. Otcu) of *Bilingual Community Education and Multilingualism: Beyond Heritage Languages in a Global City* (Multilingual Matters, 2012).

Series Editor's Preface

Colin Brock

Underlying this entire series on *Education as a Humanitarian Response* is the well known adage in education that 'if we get it right for those most in need we will likely get it right for all if we take the same approach'. That sentiment was born in relation to those with special educational needs within a full mainstream system of schooling. In relation to this series it is taken further to embrace not only the special educational needs of those experiencing disasters and their aftermath, whether natural or man made, but also to other groups who may be significantly disadvantaged. Indeed, much can be learned of value to the provision of mainstream systems from the holistic approach that necessarily follows in response to situations of disaster. Sadly very little of this potential value is actually perceived, and even less is embraced. Consequently one of the aims of the series, both in the core volume *Education as a Global Concern*, and the contributing volumes, is to bring the notion of education as a humanitarian response to the mainstream, and those seeking to serve it as teachers, other educators, and politicians.

The situation of disadvantaged children and young people is one where this approach is most strikingly illustrated in terms of the disconnect between rhetoric and reality. The number of the young disadvantaged massively outnumbers those subject to natural disasters, and even those caught up with violent conflict and its aftermath, though some of the cases in this book are in this category. The vast majority of the young disadvantaged suffer from the inadequacies of mainstream provision or, in poorer countries, to its incompleteness.

In this volume, Mitsuko Matsumoto has gathered a range of examples of educational disadvantage among children and young people in very different contexts in both industrialised and developing countries. The variety of responses to the educational needs described is itself instructive of the degree of innovation required. Non-formal and informal dimensions of education are to the fore, sometimes even within the formal setting itself, or in relation to it. The children and young people who are the subject of the chapters in this volume are a significant part of what I have described as the 'marginalized majority' in the introductory book to this series *Education as a Global Concern* (2011). They are largely overlooked in the literature of comparative and international education, that deals the mainstream, and that of education in emergencies. Mitsuko Matsumoto has offered us a series of rare insights into their worlds and the efforts of innovative educators to meet their particular humanitarian needs.

Colin Brock
Senior Research Fellow in Comparative
and International Education
University of Oxford, UK

Acknowledgements

I am very thankful to all the contributors of this volume. They have produced unique chapters, shedding light on education and disadvantaged children and young people from different angles. In addition, they showed great understanding and were responsive to the time constraints and the suggestions made. I am also very grateful to Dr Colin Brock, the *Education as a Humanitarian Response* series editor. Throughout the whole process he has lent me a kind of support that was much beyond his 'duty' as a series editor.

I am thankful to Dr Brock also for asking me to edit a volume on education and disadvantaged children and young people. The primary reason I decided to go into the field of education was because I have been convinced of its potential to empower the disadvantaged and the suffering to improve their lives and to establish a lasting happiness, and this book is exactly about it. I have grown up in and identify myself with Soka education, which centres on the idea that education is for the sake of learners' happiness and a *good* education is a way to fundamentally empower the weak, thereby making the world a better place. The founder of Soka education, Tsunesaburo Makiguchi, himself dedicated to improve education for the poor children, as a school teacher and a principal in pre-Second World War Japan.

I would like to dedicate this volume *Education and Disadvantaged Children and Young People* to Tsunesaburo Makiguchi and to Daisaku Ikeda, who made Makiguchi's visions into reality by establishing a Soka education system.

Mitsuko Matsumoto

Introduction

Mitsuko Matsumoto

Chapter Outline

This volume attempts to address the issue of disadvantage in education. It is about various groups of children and young people who are marginalized from or disadvantaged in the school system, that is, those who have no or little educational opportunities and/or with low quality. The volume comprises case studies from around the world to introduce the reader to the issue, and to ponder how it can be redressed. It is the contention of the volume and the series *Education as a Humanitarian Response* that countering disadvantage in education faced by groups of children and young people around the world is a humanitarian response.

This introductory chapter has four components. First, a global overview of the situation; second, a brief portrait of aspects of the problem in Sierra Leone, one of the poorest countries; third, the main objectives and approach of the book; and fourth, a brief introduction to its component chapters.

Global overview

By 2008, 67 million children were still out of school, although the number has fallen remarkably over the past decade (UNESCO, 2010). In 26 countries – mostly low-income countries – 20 per cent or more of those aged 17–22 have fewer than 2 years of schooling, and in some countries, including Burkina Faso and Somalia, the share has increased to 50 per cent or more (UNESCO, 2010). Achieving a high enrolment rate at the national level does not necessarily mean that all the children have equal opportunities to and in education; for instance, in India (which Sidiqqui discusses in the volume) the primary adjusted Net Enrolment Rate (NER)[1] was 95.5 per cent in 2008 (UNESCO, 2011) and the average number of years of education was over 11 years for the richest 20 per cent (UNESCO, 2010). Yet, the average number of years of schooling for the poorest 20 per cent was below 5 years and was even worse for poor female children in Bihar, a state in northern India – less than 2 years (UNESCO, 2010). Educationally disadvantaged children are not only found in developing countries; they are numerous in the developed countries too. For instance, in the United States – which Hantzopoulos takes up in this volume – the bottom 10 per cent of performers score below the average for Thailand and Tunisia in the Trends in International Mathematics and Science Study (TIMSS) scale (UNESCO, 2010). Further, there is a significant variation in the high school graduation rate by race there – while that for white students is 84 per cent, for Hispanics, it falls to 72 per cent and for African American students, it is further lower at 65 per cent (UNESCO, 2010).

In 2010, the Education for All (EFA) Global Monitoring Report (GMR), annually published by UNESCO, has taken up educationally disadvantaged children and young people as the central issue. Titled 'Reaching the Marginalised', the report argues that '[t]ackling marginalisation [in education] is a matter of urgency' (UNESCO, 2010, p. 136). Clearly, the EFA targets adopted in the Dakar Framework of Action (UNESCO, 2000), including universal primary education by 2015, will not be achieved unless the extremely disadvantaged children who are currently out of school are provided with opportunities to attend school (UNESCO, 2010). The GMR 2010 also argues that extreme and persistent disadvantage in education is detrimental both to individuals and to societies. Lack of, scarce or limited schooling can lead to little chances for socio-economic mobility. Indeed, it widens and deepens the inequalities in society. Not providing access to education to everyone also means, according to the GMR 2010 (UNESCO, 2010), a waste of skills, talent and opportunities for growth and innovation, given the present even more knowledge-based global economy. It is a stark example of 'clearly remediable injustice' (UNESCO, 2010, p. 135); disadvantaged children are not provided with educational opportunities that are enshrined in the Universal Declaration of Human Rights (United Nations, 1948).

Such educational disadvantage is not solely about lack of *provision* of schooling. As Hantzopoulos and Parker in this volume discuss, the disadvantaged groups often lack motivations to (continue to) go to schools even when opportunities are provided. Further, disadvantage is about the quality of schooling, achievement in schools and the economic and social returns of schooling that the disadvantaged exhibit in the wiser society (e.g., UNESCO, 2010; Klasen, 2001). In Peru, indigenous people have not only had far less access to education than the *mestizo* or the white population, but have also had significantly lower returns on their education (measured as additional income earned from education) (e.g., Figueroa, 2008).

Who are disadvantaged in education then? It is not easy and may not even be appropriate to define or categorize disadvantaged children and young people universally. Educational disadvantage can be approached from multiple angles, for example, access, quality, achievements and returns. In addition, as this book will show, and as the GMR 2010 recognizes, the interactions of various factors, different from one context to another, create and reinforce cycles of educational disadvantage. There is no case study on Sierra Leone in the book, but in the section below, that country is used to exemplify the wide range of disadvantaged children and young people and the complex interrelations of factors that make them educationally disadvantaged.

The case of Sierra Leone

Sierra Leone experienced a decade-long civil war (1991–2002). Not only is it still struggling to fully recover from the damages that the conflict has brought to the country, but it is also one of the poorest countries in the world. The country ranks as the 180th country out of 187 countries in the Human Development Index (UNDP, 2011), with USD 340 Gross National Income per capita (Atlas method) in 2010 (World Bank, 2011). Based on this context, Sierra Leonean children can be said to be disadvantaged in general. Many of the young people who spent their childhoods during the war had lost the chance to go to school and several studies found that school-age children still suffer from the trauma (e.g., Pessima et al., 2009). Furthermore, the general quality of public schooling is low, largely due to the weak capacity of the state and the educational system. Classrooms are grossly overcrowded, with the majority having at least 80 pupils. Many children rely only on the limited subject knowledge of the teachers. They cannot afford textbooks, and to make the matter worse, the pupils are forced to buy 'pamphlets' on subjects that teachers prepare and sell in order to augment their own meagre incomes. The extremely low quality is also apparent in the abysmal public examination results, particularly those in the West African Senior School Certificate Examination (WASSCE), taken at the end of the senior secondary school (SSS) (see Table 1.1 below). The pass rate in 2009 was less than 4 per cent for both male and female candidates. Not only has the pass rate declined considerably since the year 2000, near the end of the civil war, but these results were worse than other countries in Anglophone West Africa, where WASSCE is a standardized test.

Not only are Sierra Leonean children generally disadvantaged in education, some groups of children are more so than others. This is particularly evident at the higher level of schooling. While the enrolment to primary school has greatly improved after the war, with the Gross Enrolment Rate in 2004 being 104 per cent[2] (Dupigny et al., 2006), only half of Class 1 pupils are expected to reach Class 6, and only about 30 per cent reach the last year of basic education (i.e., junior secondary school, Year 3) (World Bank, 2007). Obviously, children from the poorest families, and orphans and street children have the most difficulty in making and maintaining contact with a school. The World Bank (2007) showed that the SSS enrolment rate of children whose families are among the poorest 20 per cent is only 11 per cent of that of children whose families are among the richest 20 per cent. In-school and out-of-school young people in the writer's own research explained that poverty and lack of parental support were the reasons why children in Sierra Leone drop out from schooling

Table 1.1 Pass rate (%) for WASSCE in 2000, 2005, and 2009 in Sierra Leone[1]

	Male	Female
2000	26.9	10.6
2005	5.2	3.3
2009	3.8	2.9

[1] The WASSCE pass in the table indicates achieving credits in four or more subjects.

Source: West African Research Council, Freetown.

(Matsumoto, 2012). Although fees for attending primary school have been abolished, there are still indirect costs, such as for uniforms, textbooks, 'pamphlets' and for the 'extra' classes that teachers give outside the regular school hours. It has been estimated to cost as much as USD 39.15 per child per year at primary level in Sierra Leone (UNICEF, 2009). At the secondary level, for the few that are able to enrol, there are fees to be paid. Many parents find the opportunity cost of sending their children to school not worthwhile in the interests of family survival.

Locality also matters. Children in rural areas in the northern region are particularly educationally disadvantaged. Historically, the development of schooling in Sierra Leone had been concentrated on urban areas (see, for instance, Riddell, 1970). Although it improved after the civil war, the enrolment rate to SSS in the rural areas is only about one-fifth of that in the urban areas (World Bank, 2007). The development of schooling in the northern region has always lagged behind compared to other regions. Modern schooling came to Sierra Leone together with Christianity from the coastal zone, as in other West African countries. In the interior north, a strong Muslim influence retained their traditional religious schools. The enrolment rate to SSS in the northern region of Sierra Leone is only 14 per cent of that in the West, which includes the capital, Freetown, and the Krio community that benefited from post-emancipation support from the nineteenth century (World Bank, 2007).

Gender is also an additional factor that reinforces educational disadvantage in Sierra Leone (Brock and Cammish, 1997). For example, the family of Musu,[3] who lives in Makeni city in the northern region, did not send her to junior secondary school because they concentrated all the resources they had to send her eldest brother to the University of Sierra Leone in Freetown. Another informant, Mabinty, withdrew from school due to the war and never returned as her family wanted her to remain at home, doing chores and minding her siblings. Girls from remote villages who had to commute long distances to school were found to be very likely to drop out due to becoming pregnant by men who offer transport in exchange for sex. As in the rural regions elsewhere, but even more so, a high proportion of girls, and families as a whole, remain marginalized as far as educational and many other opportunities are concerned.

The case of Sierra Leone has been briefly reviewed here because it exemplifies the situation for children and young people for the marginalized majority of the rural and urban poor of the so-called developing world (Brock, 2011).

The objectives and approach of the volume

Against this backdrop, the objectives of the book are threefold:

1. to develop a contextualized understanding of disadvantaged children and young people with regard to education;
2. to deepen the understanding of factors that fuel educational disadvantage; and
3. to learn from some success stories how their disadvantage has been redressed.

The focus and style of the book is not to go deeply into theoretical debates as to defining what disadvantage in education is, or how to measure it. Nor is it to thoroughly study the issues that make some groups of children and young people disadvantaged in education in one national or regional context, as some other books have done (e.g., Cox, 2000). Rather, being part of the series *Education as a Humanitarian Response*, the book attempts to begin to address educational disadvantage holistically and globally by focusing on a range of particular cases and situations.

Attempting to understand the educationally disadvantaged children does not mean trying to come up with a universal categorization of them. Categorization can be useful in some contexts, as in India, as Siddiqui shows in Chapter 4, for affirmative actions to be taken for certain groups of children. And yet, 'context matters' (Crossley, 2001). As will be apparent, different groups of children or young people are disadvantaged in each context, and the issues that hinder them from schooling or create disadvantage in schooling are both particular and diverse. As O'Higgins and Evans demonstrate in Chapter 3, these children may refuse to be categorized as such, fearing maltreatment from their peers and also simply desiring to be treated equal to others.

The underlying epistemology of the volume is that the disadvantaged children and young people themselves can be engaged directly in research and that their voice matters. This has often been neglected in educational research. Given the diverse focus of the chapters in a limited space, not all chapters incorporate the voices of the children and young people, but some, especially Hantzopoulos, O'Higgins and Evans and Parker, directly engage with disadvantaged pupils and show that they are capable of expressing their perspectives about schooling and providing relevant data on the issue.

In addition to developing the contextualized understanding of disadvantaged children and young people in respect of education, the book attempts to show successful initiatives that have been able to go some way to redress particular disadvantages. For example, the use of sports in this regard is exemplified.

Each chapter has a different focus and operates on a different scale. Some are approaching overviews, while others are very specific in their spatial focus. All aim to illustrate aspects of educational responses to humanitarian needs.

The chapters

Chapter 1 is about an alternative school, Humanities Preparatory Academy, in New York, United States, by Maria Hantzopoulos. The school successfully engages with disadvantaged pupils from high-poverty backgrounds and historically marginalized populations. Drawing on her research there, Hantzopoulos focuses on the role that the student–teacher relationships play in the school's success. She shows how students themselves perceive their relationships with teachers to be exceptional, and delineates the key characteristics of those relationships.

In Chapter 2, Zeena Zakharia takes up a Shi`i school in Lebanon as a case that effectively engages with children and young people who are disadvantaged historically and also by violent conflict. Shi`a are historically marginalized in Lebanon, and further, they have been deeply affected by the 2006 July war and sustained insecurity afterwards. Having collected ethnographic data in the 2006–2007 academic year, she shows how the school addressed both direct and structural violence (social injustice), using a community-centred approach.

Like Hantzopoulos, Aoife O'Higgins and Rosalind Evans in Chapter 3 centre on the perspectives and experiences of disadvantaged children and young people. They discuss educational issues and the experiences of migrant children and young people in the United Kingdom. Based on research projects that The Children's Society has facilitated with young migrants, they show the considerable extent to which they value educational opportunities, despite the barriers they face in accessing formal education. They also emphasize the young migrants' strong wish not to be singled out by their immigration status, and the importance of this to be taken into account in determining the approach to support them.

Chapter 4 is an overview of educational conditions that surround disadvantaged children in India. Mohammad Akhtar Siddiqui discusses the educational conditions and the national responses to each of the six major categories of disadvantaged children who constitute the majority of out-of-school children in India – children of Scheduled Castes and Tribes, Muslims, migrant workers, urban deprived children, children with special needs and girls. He concludes with the importance not only of ensuring the access of these children to elementary education, but also ensuring the quality of education that they could receive, highlighting teachers as the primary factor that can make a difference.

The following chapter, Chapter 5, by Margaryta Danilko and Nadiya Ivanenko is also a national overview – the case of Ukraine. They discuss the range of disadvantaged children and young people in that country and the initiatives that are presently in place to support them. They identify the disadvantaged as street children, trafficked children, children specifically affected by the Chernobyl disaster, orphans in general and children in orphanages and *internats*. They describe and discuss a number of policies and programmes operated on different scales, from national, regional to local, as well as those run by various non-governmental organizations (NGOs).

Chapters 6 and 7 focus on the role that sports can play in helping disadvantaged children and young people. Parker Goyer discusses how her initiative and NGO, *Coach for College*, operates in rural Vietnam by helping poor rural children remain in school long enough to connect with post-school opportunities. *Coach for College* provides a mix of sports and academic support during the vacations. Goyer shows how the programme motivates children to stay in school in the short-term as well as promotes long-term benefits, such as their psychological well-being and the acquisition of relevant skills.

The last chapter, Chapter 7, is about Commonwealth Games Canada's approach and programmes in the Caribbean and Africa, using sports as a means to promote development and a culture of peace. Colin Higgs, Carla Thachuk, Hannah Juneau, Rachael Kalaba and Natalie Brett describe three different paradigms that exist with regard to sport, among which they follow a paradigm in which sport is intentionally used for the sake of development and peace. Along with some examples from the programmes in Africa and the Caribbean, which they operate to help disadvantaged children, they present a conceptual framework on which their programmes are based.

The book closes with a short conclusion, synthesizing the insights provided by the case studies in the volume about education and disadvantaged children and young people.

Notes

1 Net Enrolment Ratio (NER) means the rate of enrolment of the official age group of children for a level of education. Primary adjusted NER includes primary school-aged children who are enrolled in secondary schools as well as in primary schools (e.g., UNESCO, 2010).

2 This number surpasses 100 per cent because children older than the official age group of children tend to be enrolled in schools in African countries, including Sierra Leone, and the GER is calculated as the ratio of total enrolment *regardless of age* to the population of *the age group* that officially corresponds to the level of education.

3 For ethical reasons, I use pseudonyms for names of participants in my study, and all the details regarding my study referred in this chapter can be found in Matsumoto, 2011 and 2012.

References

Brock, C. (2011). *Education As a Global Concern.* London: Continuum Books.

Brock, C. and Cammish, N. K. (1997). *Factors Affecting Female Participation in Education in Seven Developing Countries.* London: DfID.

Cox, T. (ed.) (2000). *Combating Educational Disadvantage: Meeting the Needs of Vulnerable Children.* New York: Falmer Press.

Crossley, M. (2001). Introduction: Context Matters. *Comparative Education* 37(4): 405–8.

Dupigny, A. C., Kargbo, I. G. and Yallancy, A. (2006). *2004 Population and Housing Census: Analytical Report on Education and Literacy.* Statistics Sierra Leone. [Online]. Available from: <http://www.statistics.sl/2004%20Pop.%20&%20Hou.%20Census%20Analytical%20Reports/2004%20Population%20and%20Housing%20Census%20Report%20on%20Education%20and%20Literacy.pdf> (Accessed 30 November 2009).

Figueroa, A. (2008). *Education, Labour Markets and Inequality in Peru.* Centre for Research on Inequality, Human Security and Ethnicity. Available from: <http://www.crise.ox.ac.uk/pubs/workingpaper48.pdf> (Accessed 13 January 2011).

Klasen, S. (2001). Social Exclusion, Children and Education: Implications of a Rights-based Approach. *European Societies* 3(4): 413–45.

Matsumoto, M. (2012). *Education and the Risk of Violent Conflict in Low-Income and Weak States, with Special Reference to Schooling: The Case of Sierra Leone.* DPhil thesis, Oxford: University of Oxford.

—(2011). Expectations and Realities of Education in Post-Conflict Sierra Leone: A Reflection of Society or a Driver for Peacebuilding? In J. Paulson (ed.), *Education, Conflict and Development.* Oxford: Symposium Books, pp. 119–44.

Pessima, A., Macauley, C., Lebbie, M., Manley, J. and Buck, R. E. (2009). *Trauma Healing of Victims of Sierra Leone's 10-year Civil War: A Needs Intervention Study Based on Personal Testimonies of Selected Victims.* Bamako: Education Research Network for West and Central Africa.

Riddell, J. B. (1970). *The Spatial Dynamics of Modernization in Sierra Leone: Structure, Diffusion, and Response.* Evanston, IL: Northwestern University Press.

UNDP (2011). *Human Development Report 2011: Sustainability and Equity; A Better Future for All.* New York: UNDP.

UNESCO (2011). *EFA Global Monitoring Report 2011: The Hidden Crisis; Armed Conflict and Education.* Paris: UNESCO.

—(2010). *EFA Global Monitoring Report 2010: Reaching the Marginalized.* Paris: UNESCO.

—(2000). *Dakar Framework for Action: Education for All; Meeting Our Collective Commitments.* Paris: UNESCO.

UNICEF (2009). *Out-of-school Children of Sierra Leone.* UNICEF. [Online]. Available from: <http://www.educationfasttrack.org/media/library/Final_Out_of_School_Study_Sierra_Leone_012009.pdf> (Accessed 1 May 2010).

United Nations (1948). *Universal Declaration of Human Rights.* New York: United Nations.

World Bank (2011). *World Bank Development Report 2011: Conflict, Security, and Development.* Washington D.C.: World Bank.

—(2007). *Education in Sierra Leone: Present Challenges, Future Opportunities.* Washington D.C.: World Bank.

1

Building Relationships to Engage At-Risk Youth: A Case Study of a New York City Public High School

Maria Hantzopoulos

Chapter Outline

In 2006, the U.S. public policy think tank Civic Enterprises released the report *The Silent Epidemic: Perspectives of High School Dropouts* to bring attention to the increasing dropout rates of high school students in the United States. Though many people were astounded to learn that almost one-third of American public school students do not complete high school, the rates for African American, Latino, and Native American youth were even higher at almost 50 per cent (Bridgeland et al., 2006; 2009). After uncovering and clarifying the circumstances that contribute to dropout rates in their report, the authors urged for multipronged educational policy reforms emanating from national, state, local, and school community levels to address the needs of the youth. Further, while they implored policy makers to keep dropout rates at the center of their reform efforts, they insisted on viewing youth on the verge of dropping out not "as problems to be solved, but as potential to be fulfilled" (p. 20).

Despite these suggestions that multiple and multilevel actors need to be included in school reform, U.S. public educational policy continues to be top-down, as manifested in the proliferating large-scale federal reforms "No Child Left Behind" and "Race to the Top." Shaped by rhetoric that demonizes public schools, their teachers, and their students, the discourses surrounding these policies contribute to a notion of "failure" that suggests that public schools are incapable of preparing and educating children. While ostensibly designed to remedy public schools, these reforms, in reality, have been the real failure—their emphasis on "accountability" through high stakes testing on these exams have only exacerbated existing inequities, including dropout rates, in schools (Arbuthnot, 2011; McNeil et al., 2011). By placing primacy on test scores and school performance above all other educational matters, these initiatives create pressure on teachers and schools to prepare their students solely for the tests at the expense of other empirically sound effective pedagogies. Further, these testing policies come with high stakes for both the students and the schools as failure to meet specific achievement targets among students could result in closure, administrative and curricular changes, and/or loss of school funding (see Karp, 2006). Not only do these top-down policies overlook important research about successful approaches to engaging students in school, they also ignore what teachers, students, and school communities say are effective pedagogical practices that redress dropout rates and re-socialize students academically.

There is a plethora of research, however, that shows how concepts such as strong student–teacher relationships, positive school culture, and an engaging academic curricula can improve and address inequities in schooling (Antorp-Gonzalez, 2011; Bajaj, 2009; Bartlett and Koyama, 2012; Bartlett and Garcia, 2011; de Jesús, 2012; Hantzopoulos, 2011a; 2011b; 2012a; 2012b; Rivera-McCutchen, 2012; Rodriguez and Conchas, 2008; Shiller, 2012; Tyner-Mullings, 2012). This chapter builds upon this existing literature, specifically elucidating the importance of relationship-building in addressing inequities in schooling. I draw from two years of ethnographic data collection at a "critical" small high school in New York City (see Hantzopoulos, 2009; Hantzopoulos and Tyner-Mullings, 2012) to shed light on how former and current students make meaning of their experiences at a school, Humanities Preparatory Academy (Prep), which emphasizes strong student–teacher relationships. Drawing from interviews and anecdotal surveys, I demonstrate how the school effectively engaged students academically through these relationships when many of these students were close to abandoning the school project all together.

The chapter advances these current conversations about student–teacher relationships by placing the youth perspective at the center, addressing a gap in the literature that presently does not always pay attention to how students describe and understand these relationships. In particular, I reveal the specific qualities that youth ascribe to their relationships with their teachers and provide a more complete picture about the role that these played in their academic trajectory. While there are several other practices and structures at this school that contribute to the students' academic re-socialization (see Hantzopoulos 2011b; 2012a; 2012b), I demonstrate in this chapter how the youth viewed these relationships as tantamount to their experience. Thus, I will conclude by stating that macroeducational policies cannot overlook the importance of relationship-building as one of several features in authentic school reform, both as a way to ameliorate schools and to remedy dropout rates.

Dropping out and staying in: A brief review

The subject of school dropouts has been explored from a variety of perspectives, including social, cultural, psychological, and economic variables. Scholars such as Rumberger (2004) have argued that individual factors (i.e., race, socioeconomic status, gender etc . . .) and structural factors (i.e., poverty, community, family, etc . . .) can exacerbate the risk factors for students, increasing the likelihood of dropping out. While these intersecting factors certainly contribute to reasons for dropping out, studies have also shown that there are certain school environmental conditions that increase dropout rates. According to Suh and Suh (2007), one of the main predictors of dropping out of school is a previous suspension history. Based on a large-scale longitudinal study, they found that if students had a history of suspension, the likelihood of that student dropping out increased by 78 per cent (Suh and

Suh, 2007; Lee et al., 2011). While student behavior certainly can contribute to disciplinary measures such as suspension, research also shows that the school climate and culture contributes to suspension rates. Scholars such as Fine (1991), Bowditch (1993), and Fergusen (2001) have shown through ethnographic studies the ways in which students—particularly students of color—are, in fact, criminalized in their school environments and perceived as "trouble." As studies repeatedly show that schools with excessively punitive disciplinary policies and high suspension rates have higher dropout rates (see Suh and Suh, 2007; Christle et al., 2007), many scholars and youth advocates prefer the term "push out" to describe the phenomenon of students leaving school (National Economic and Social Rights Initiative, 2007; New York Civil Liberties Union, 2009).

Several studies also show that the emphasis on high-stakes testing contributes to increased dropout rates, particularly for students of color, multilingual students, and those with diagnosed disabilities (Amrein and Berliner, 2003; Arbuthnot, 2011; Futrell and Rotberg, 2002; Hayward, 2002; Horn, 2003; Katsyiannis et al., 2007; Marchant, 2004; Maudaus and Clarke, 2001; McNeil et al., 2011; Menken, 2008; Vasquez-Heilig and Darling-Hammond, 2008). While they cite a variety of factors that affect students' performance on theses tests (including cultural biases, language ability, access to supplementary resources, etc . . .), most argue that the unintended consequences of these exams outweigh the benefits. Further, high-stakes testing often works in tandem with zero-tolerance disciplinary measures, and many argue that the two are inextricably linked to create higher dropout rates. As the latter criminalizes students for minor infractions of school rules, the former encourages administrators to push out students who do not improve their schools' overall test scores (Advancement Project, 2011; American Civil Liberties Union, 2010). Despite documentation of these negative outcomes, over-testing and over-policing in schools permeate the broader school reform agenda in the United States.

Conversely, other studies illuminate certain school practices and structures that can help students stay *in* school. For instance, these studies illustrate how a positive school culture can lower the suspension rates through prevention strategies that aim to reduce inappropriate behaviors. These strategies include increasing parental involvement in school-based discipline plans, emphasizing student needs in educational planning, and creating a culture of mutual respect (Christle et al., 2004; Mukuria, 2002; Raffaele-Mendez, Knoff, and Ferron, 2002). Moreover, scholars have pointed to the importance of relationships in creating a positive school culture. According to Lesser et al. (2008), moments of feeling cared for by teachers can have a profound impact on whether or not students actually drop out of school. Based on their research that tracked how dropouts prolonged their stay in school, they found that when these students were acknowledged and valued by their teachers, they felt happier and were more willing to stay in school. In addition, several scholars have written about the role that student–teacher relationships play in make the school a welcoming and inviting place, particularly for those that may be "at risk" for dropping out (see Antorp-Gonzalez, 2011; Bajaj, 2009; Bartlett and Koyama, 2012; Bartlett and Garcia, 2011; de Jesús, 2012; Hantzopoulos, 2011b; 2012a; 2012b; Rivera-McCutchen, 2012; Rodriguez and Conchas, 2008; Tyner-Mullings, 2012).

In a recent response article about why students drop out of school, Rodriguez (2010) urges reformers to consider the impact of school policies (such as zero-tolerance, rigid testing, etc. . .) on the creation of a culture of respect and intellectual engagement. While he acknowledges that there is often little that schools can do to mitigate external factors (such as poverty) that contribute to dropout rates, he suggests that schools can undertake some actions that will help students stay in school. In particular, he implores reformers to (1) forge dialogues about school culture, (2) create forums for student voices, and (3) focus on relationships between the teachers and students (p. 19). This runs concordant with the suggestions made by advocacy organizations such as the National Economic and Social Rights Initiative and the New York Civil Liberties Union.

In many ways, Prep, the school where I conducted my research, adopts this multipronged approach to school reform. As I demonstrate elsewhere, there were several processes and structures at Prep, including the transmission of core values, the democratic school structures, and the participatory nature of the school curriculum that contributed to positive student academic and social experiences at the school (see Hantzopoulos, 2011b; 2012a; 2012b). This chapter, however, looks more closely at the role that student–teacher relationships played in this effort, shedding light on the characteristics that contributed to an overall sense of belonging for students, which helped them stay in and succeed in school.

Humanities Preparatory Academy[1]

Prep was originally founded as a program in a larger comprehensive New York City public high school that sought to re-engage students who were potentially at-risk for dropping out. The goal of the program was not just to keep them in school, but also to help prepare them for life beyond graduation, including college. Utilizing innovative and democratic pedagogies, intellectually and socially relevant curicula, and personalized approaches to student–teacher relationships, Prep was extremely successful with this population and eventually became an autonomous public school. While the school presently serves a mixed population of those that may have had previous "success" in schools and those that have struggled, it continues to attempt to reach all students "by personalizing our learning situations, by democratizing and humanizing the school environment, and by creating a 'talking culture,' an atmosphere of informal intellectual discourse among students and faculty" (School Mission). By constructing an alternative educational environment rooted in democracy, public intellectualism, and caring school practices, Prep presents itself as a place that provides a transformative experience for its students, both within and beyond the sphere of the school. It remains rather small for a New York City high school (under 180 students) and is crammed into two corridors of a larger educational facility.

The school's demographic composition reflects the racial and economic spectrum of New York City. In 2006–2007, the year in which I conducted most of my research, students identified as follows: 40 per cent Latino, 38 per cent Black, 12 per cent White, 6 per cent Asian, and 4 per cent Other. Twelve per cent received mandated services for special education, which was slightly above the city average of 11 per cent. This percentage does not include de-certified students who were still receiving some auxiliary services from the school. Approximately 54 per cent qualified for free and reduced lunch, though the administration of Prep estimates this as much higher; high school students do not often submit the requisite forms that qualify them for such. The schools' graduation and college acceptance rates far surpass average New York City statistics. For example, the school had between 91 per cent and 100 per cent college acceptance rates since it opened in 1997 while the city-wide rate never went above 62 per cent in any of these years, as documented by the New York Performance Standards Consortium. The dropout rate has been consistently under 4 per cent as opposed to the New York Department of Education documented city rate of 19.9 per cent.

Building strong student–teacher relationships: The elements of transformation

Current and former students at Prep overwhelmingly describe the relationships with teachers and other adults in the school as positive and exceptionally different from anything they have previously experienced. For these students, these relationships contribute to shaping an overall encouraging school experience at Prep, despite having had a lack of enthusiasm about school previously. While some students are vague in their descriptions, simply stating, as Victor[2] did, that "you get a closer relationship with all the students and teachers" (Interview, 20 May 2007), most students distinguish particular qualities that make these relationships unique. As a result, several themes emerge from these descriptions, including: teachers as equals; a culture of trust; a culture of care; the concept of family; and teachers as friends. While several of these themes overlap and reinforce each other, they clearly demarcate specific characteristics of positive relationship-building between the students and teachers.

Teacher as "Equals"

One of the central ways in which students describe their relationships with teachers is as egalitarian. For instance, Franz, an alumnus, writes the following in a survey that asks him to summarize his experience at Prep: "The teacher/student boundaries were blurred, and the teachers learned as much from the students as the students did from them." He suggests that not only do students gain from this relational paradigm shift, but that teachers do as well. In many ways, this statement is evocative of the vision Freire (1972/2003) beheld for student–teacher relationships, in which hierarchies are flattened and knowledge is co-constructed and shared. Antonia, another alumna, also notes the effects of these horizontal relationships on her school experience by stating the following in her survey:

> Prep became my family when I felt I had no one at home. I feel that my teachers were my equal, not so much of an authority figure, which made me want to excel and make them proud . . . (Survey, N.d.)

For her, the flattened nature of these relationships not only contribute to a sense of belonging (by being familial), but also fuel a sense of academic accountability that is catalyzed by her commitment to her teachers and her community.

Moreover, students suggest that the ability to call teachers by their first names reinforce the idea of reciprocity between students and teachers. While many of them express being at first unaccustomed to this practice, most speak very fondly of it and acknowledge that it diminishes the traditional hierarchical structures that pervade most school environments. Luis, an alumnus and current student at Hunter College, also points to how this type of exchange reinterprets what is traditionally meant by "student":

> Like, they're (other schools) definitely lacking in . . . teacher–student relationships. I thought it was great that I was able to call my teachers by their first name. You know, because it made their relationship more personal and it made it more . . . a one on one thing rather than, you know, you're just a student in the class (Interview, 13 March 2007).

Since he is no longer engaging as "just a student in the class," but rather in a "one on one thing," Luis suggests that the first-name policy at Prep indeed helps to create a sense of equal status with teachers. Rather than just being a subordinate student to a teacher, he intimates that his humanity and individuality is recognized. These experiences run concurrent with Freirean notions of student–teacher relationships, in which the transformation presumably yields a more humanizing experience for the students (Freire, 1972/2003). Additionally, Luis positions Prep as different from other schools, intimating that the relationships at Prep interrupt the alienating processes between students and teachers that are seemingly intrinsic to traditional schooling.

A culture of trust between students and teachers

Students often describe their teachers as "trusting," and subsequently, students indicate that this makes them feel acknowledged as agents and decision makers in their own education. For instance, Lulu, a transfer student, distinguishes Prep from her old school in her survey by saying that "the overall difference between Prep and my old school is that I have more freedom to shape my education and responsibility in the choices I make." For Epiphany, an incoming ninth grader at the time of research, this act of trust manifests in simply being allowed to go out to lunch, something that very few public high school students in New York City are allowed to do. While this seems rather mundane and simple, it is a gesture that can inspire confidence in students. As Chakasia, a transfer student who was previously labeled as truant, notes:

> Prep has taught me to be more responsible in a way because in my other schools, I never went out to lunch or anything like that, so just me coming back, that tells me a lot about myself, cause I could just go home and stuff like that. But I come back, so, in a way, it's made me more responsible and more mature I would say (Focus Group, 9 May 2007).

By having choices and decision-making power, students intimate that they feel more responsible. In many ways, this description dovetails with notions of "critical care," a theory that suggests that high expectations in a nurturing environment leads to increased confidence and academic achievement among students, particularly students of color (Antrop-Gonzalez and de Jesús, 2005; Rodriguez and Conchas, 2008).

Other students describe how the teacher's trust translates into academic success. For example, Zack, a transfer student from another alternative school with a similar mission and population, distinguishes the two schools based on the teacher's trust:

> I feel like I got out of Prep a bigger sense of responsibility, because you have to choose your own classes, and once you choose your classes, then you really don't have the right to complain about it, because you chose that. I don't know. I feel like I am prepared to go to college, or into some other higher form of education. Before, when I went to [School X] . . . well, they call themselves an alternative school, but really, there's really not much alternative about it. You . . . basically have your classes that they give you. You stay in the same class with the same people. You go and you learn what you learn, and that's what you learn, and that's it . . . I like Prep because you just . . . get to choose your classes . . . the things you want to learn, and I think that's cool (Focus Group, 4 May 2007).

Thus, the level of curricular choice (within the parameters of state guidelines) not only renders a sense of responsibility and maturity in the students, but also a feeling of being trusted by their teachers. In turn, the emphasis on student decision-making contributes to successful academic re-engagement of students, as they feel responsible for the actions and choices they are making.

A culture of care

Another explicit way students describe their relationships with teachers are as ones embedded with care, and in particular, the previously defined concept of "critical care." Studies by scholars de Jesús (2012) and Valenzuela (1999) show how authentic and critical caring relationships between teachers and students translate into increased student engagement and academic success, particularly for Latino students, who have been historically and contemporarily underserved by public and Anglo-dominated educational institutions. This study is not specifically about Latino students nor is it about a Latino-centric community-based school. Nevertheless, Prep students—many of whom previously felt alienated from school—describe several characteristics of care that echo some of the ways in which caring operates within a more critical framework that seeks to redress inequities in schooling.

One common way that critical care transpires is through the ways in which teachers went beyond their pedagogical duties and check in with students. Reneka, an alumna attending college, remembers her experience:

> I mean the counselor that I went to . . . helped me when I was having problems in the house [at home with her family]. You know it was just . . . organized so you would be able to talk about stuff that's going on in your house. Teachers were really concerned (Interview, 12 March 2007).

Similarly, Jonathan, a junior who actually left Prep for a semester and then came back, states:

> I felt that the school was not really my thing. And then I realized that it was . . . a home away from home. And the reason I say that is because the teachers just concern [themselves with] everything around you. Everything that you do is their business and that's a good thing . . . if you do something wrong, they don't look over you for it. And they're just going to make sure it's all right. You know, to make sure that you're doing fine and they check in with you every step of the way to make sure you're doing a-okay (Focus Group, 11 May 2007).

The way in which Jonathan describes *how* teachers cared is evocative of a "critical care" approach as teachers take interest in students' lives, but also hold the students accountable for their actions, in supportive ways.

For some students, this type of care and interest translates into raising expectations for themselves. For example, Mattias, a senior, explains in a focus group:

> It's given me opportunity, cause you know before I came to this school, I wasn't that kind of good kid or whatever . . . I wasn't at all. I was trouble-doomed or whatever. I feel like coming to this school, everybody's so nice to each other,

> especially if you have the teachers who really care about you, you start to realize, you know, the teachers are going fifty [meet you halfway] with you so you may as well put the other fifty in to complete the circle . . . (18 May 2007).

Mattias describes how the teachers' expectations of him, coupled with "niceness" and care, encourage him to be his best self. Despite describing his previous self as "doomed," Mattias graduated shortly after this research and won a prestigious four-year leadership scholarship to a competitive liberal arts college. These heightened expectations ostensibly helped him shift his own perception of himself (from "trouble" to "good kid") as a student. As Serena, a recent transfer, notes, this care boosts her esteem: "I guess the bottom line is that the teachers in Prep are . . . they care. I mean, they give you a sense of . . . confidence" (Focus Group, 4 May 2007).

In addition, Prep students and alumni explain how these high expectations make them feel validated as contributors to knowledge production. For example, Epiphany, a ninth grader, describes her transition from middle school to high school when talking about Prep teachers:

> The teachers here . . . they're very understanding . . . my old teachers, if you said something to them that they didn't like, they would give you a detention, an in-house or whatever. But this school, . . . you can say, 'Oh, I think this was a boring subject,' and they [the teachers] can be like, 'Well, how can we make it better?' They actually ask you 'How can we make it better?' They actually listen to your side. They actually want to know how you want to be teached (sic). You can say, 'I learn better if we watch a movie. I learn better if we read from papers. I learn better if we just talk. I learn better if we work in groups.' They actually try to make it that so everyone learns comfortably (Interview, 23 March 2007).

Thus, the view that teachers are more understanding, and more pedagogically responsive to student needs, fuels an overall sense of academic pride and success. For students like Ray, a twelfth grader, this level of student attentiveness and personalization allows teachers to know his capabilities more.

> . . . all the teachers are really committed towards helping you achieve whatever your goal is and I think it's really helpful that they challenge and push you a lot . . . [like] Ms. Kemp in Global. I feel like I'm doing a lot of work for her class . . . well not a lot, but I'm doing work that's pretty good for her class. But even though I'm doing more than she's doing with the assignments, she still sees room for improvement. Even though I've already met her standards when she gave the assignment, she still says, 'Well, in terms of just writing period, there's things that you can do to make your writing better, so revise it like this and just

> start thinking about it like this and just keep working.' That kind of pushing and hearing that you're not as great as you think you are all the time really helps you drive yourself and want to achieve more (Interview, 22 March 2007).

In Ray's case, he explains that this attentiveness and subsequent encouragement help him realize his own academic potential in a nonthreatening way. In this sense, caring does not just reveal itself when teachers are uncritical of students, but rather, it manifests when high expectations are maintained for students in a supportive educational environment; this is suggestive of the notions of critical care (Antrop-Gonzalez and de Jesús, 2005).

Teachers as "Family"

The use of the word *family*, or familial descriptors (i.e., second home, parent, sister, etc.), came up frequently when talking to students about Prep. As Khadija, an alumna, states in her survey, "When I attended this school, I felt like I had a second family in most of the students and teachers." In many ways, this is an extension of the type of "critical care" suggested earlier, but it also suggests that the teachers and students looked out for each other in ways that one would look out for someone in their own family. For instance, Lisa, an alumna, explains how for her the student–teacher binary is dissolved at Prep through the family-like relationships:

> It's hard to find teachers in other high schools that are like Prep because they're very focused on you as an individual, they really want you to excel and it's more of like . . . let me see . . . the relationship, yeah to some extent it is teacher-student, but it's more of a family and they really genuinely care about the students so even if you do have an issue it's not like, you know, you have to worry about being reprimanded or you're going to be punished or sent to detention. It's more of like having that open communication as a student, which is really important . . . (Interview, 27 March 2007).

As mentioned in other data earlier, the level of personalization contributes to a type of "genuine" and "critical" care, and for Lisa, much like she would expect from her family. This resonates with how Valenzuela (1999), in her study of Mexican American youth, conceptualizes authentic caring relationships between students and teachers; that is, when students and teachers shared culturally bound concepts of caring, students trust that their teachers have their best interests at heart.

Similarly, other Prep students describe the familial ways in which teachers maintain strong disciplinary boundaries and nurture students at the same time. For example, Vivian explains:

> I guess like some of the way the teachers act towards me is kinda like how my mother and sister act towards me. Like if they know there's something I shouldn't be doing they're like, 'you know you shouldn't be doing that,' which is something that my sister and mom say. And, you know, if I do a good job they congratulate me and they're really nice to me and they make Prep feel like a second home (Interview, 23 May 2007).

In this case, Vivian describes how the care that manifests itself between teachers and students is akin to relationships among siblings or caregivers. Because of their age and experience, these teachers, like family members, dispense advice in a loving and concerned way. Her tone indicates that this was not patronizing, but coming from a place of love. Because teachers challenge students to think about their decisions and actions, Vivian feels cared for in a more authentic and "critical" way. Joshua, a ninth grader, explains it in similar terms:

> It's a big family and we share knowledge with each other . . . The teachers are – they're like school parents. They're like parents that teach. They push you and they push you and if you don't get the push and you don't get it and act right then they'll fail you, but they're not going to fail you for nothing . . . they also offer, like, help. Like you don't have to go up to them – you know because a lot of people don't like going up to people asking for help. They offer it to you (Focus Group, 22 March 2007).

In some ways, he describes how failure is not an option because the teachers are like parents who want their children to succeed; they set high expectations, but with a lot of encouragement and support. In this sense, the students at Prep feel that the teachers care for students' academic and emotional wellbeing as a family member would. In turn, this influences the ways in which students engage in school life.

Teachers as "Friends"

Another descriptor students use to talk about their teachers is "friends." In many ways, the characteristics ascribed to teachers as friends are similar to the characteristics of teachers as family. However, one distinction is that friendship has a more symmetrical connotation than "parent" or "older sister." For instance, Vivian, who earlier described teachers as being like family, highlights the ways "teachers are also like friends instead of just, you know, people who teach you . . ." She said when she describes the school to her friends who attend other schools, they are envious because:

> I tell them, 'Oh, I'm actually happy to get up and go to school in the morning' and I tell them that the teachers are really nice and that it's not all work, work, work with them . . . You know, we can also talk to them just as, you know, we talk to our friends (Interview, 23 May 2007).

Pedro echoes this sentiment. When asked what to keep about the school, he states "have the faculty be there for the students. It is really different from other schools. The faculty can really be . . . your teachers and your friends at the same time" (Interview, 10 May 2007).

What is interesting about these students' views is that strong student–teacher relationships are not simply about having conversations and being comfortable with teachers, but are also about feeling like an "equal partner" in the conversation. As noted earlier when discussing "first-name basis" relationships, students appreciate the seemingly equalized aspects of their relationships with teachers. In this sense, describing teachers as friends assumes that there is a degree of symmetry in the dynamics of the relationship. While some students seek advice from their teachers, which may connote a more traditional, hierarchical relationship, students also talk about seeking advice from their friends. The ways that students describe their teachers as friends, however, connote that there are genuine attempts to engender an inter-generational, authentic dialogue among all the school actors, reflecting the "democratizing and humanizing" environment that Prep seeks to cultivate in its mission. As Reneka, an alumna currently at Dillard, notes:

> They are not like teachers, they are more like friends . . . We weren't just any number in Prep – teachers actually knew your name, and when you'd see them in the hallways, they'd have a discussion with you. Not like a regular high school where teachers just walk by you, and they just call your name and take your attendance and that's about it – don't know anything about you. At Prep, they actually talk with you (Interview, 12 March 2007).

When describing her teachers as friends, Reneka does not use the expression talk "to you," but rather "with you," implying a more symmetrically perceived relationship that brings about authentic dialogue. Despite using descriptors like "teachers," she also suggests that the relationship transcends typical student–teacher ones and contrasts her experience with that of a "regular high school." Victor points out that these practices are matters of everyday, quotidian existence. For example, he states:

> I like the close relationship with the teachers the most. Because in no other school have I gone to dinner with teachers I had, or lunch, or just talked about my regular life or anything like that. So that's probably to me the best part of Prep (Interview, 10 May 2007).

Victor is referring to a common practice among some teachers at the school—they take students to lunch to discuss both their academic and personal situations.

Students also note that this type of rapport extends into scenarios beyond the school. For example, Reneka, who was quoted earlier, also suggests that the close relationships with her Prep teachers made her college professors, someone with inherently more power, "more approachable." Sebastien, a current senior, describes a similar situation, by stating that "meeting these teachers . . . I'm able to communicate with adults . . . that I have never been able to with any other kind of person before I came to this school" (Focus Group, 2 May 2007). Just as Reneka describes how her Prep relationships helped her approach her college professors, Sebastien explains how these relationships help him approach and interact with adults in general. Thus, the student–teacher relationships do not just help students do well in school, but also translate into social arenas at large.

Concluding thoughts

As suggested by the students' description of their teachers, strong student–teacher relationships are pivotal to the ways in which students experience schooling. In the case of students of Humanities Preparatory Academy, these relationships help cultivate a sense of welcoming and belonging, contributing to a positive perception and experience of school. While these relationships are not the only features that re-socialize students academically, the central role that they play in these students' experiences warrant attention. The characteristics students ascribe to these relationships not only illuminate how these relationships transpire at school, but also reveal the possibilities for public schools to be sites for transformative learning and successful educational attainment, particularly for youth who have been historically marginalized from schooling. This point is salient in a climate where educational polices are continually framed around notions of "accountability," despite research and data that repeatedly call these policies into question.

Nonetheless, it is also important to note that student–teacher relationships need to be maintained by boundaries, as the role of the teacher is ultimately to help the student achieve academic success. While students often place familial and fraternal descriptors on their teachers, they also repeatedly state that their teachers held them to high standards, both academically and socially. In this sense, the students' perspectives do not mean that teachers need simply be friends or be equal to students as adolescents. Rather, the data presented in the chapter suggests that teachers need to treat students with the same humanity that they would treat anyone in their peer group. This is ultimately what students will value and what will help them succeed.

Questions for reflection

- How did strong student–teacher relationships transpire at this school? Why were they so effective?
- What might be the barriers to creating such relationships? Why?

Notes

1 For more extensive versions of this school description, please see Hantzopoulos 2011b; 2012a; 2012b.

2 All names of students interviewed are pseudonyms.

Further reading

Antorp-Gonzalez, R. (2011). *Schools as Radical Sanctuaries: Decolonizing Urban Education through the Eyes of Youth of Color and their Teachers*. Charlotte, NC: Information Age Publishing.

This book shows how two public, urban, small schools have become "sanctuaries" for their students, their families, and communities of color. Specifically, the author shows that when pedagogy and practice is linked to community-based, culturally relevant, decolonizing, and social justice-oriented frameworks, dropout rates decrease and academic achievement increases.

Bartlett, L. and Garcia, O. (2011). *Additive Schooling in Subtractive Times: Bilingual Education and Dominican Immigrant Youth in the Heights*. Nashville, TN: Vanderbilt University Press.

This book shows how one New York City high school successfully educates Dominican immigrant youth, at a time when Latino immigrants constitute a growing and vulnerable population in the nation's secondary schools. In particular, it shows how the community responds to the linguistic and social challenges it faces through an "additive" and care-centered approach.

Fine, M. (1991). *Framing Dropouts: Notes on the Politics of an Urban Public High School*. Albany: State University of New York.

This is a classic school ethnography that shows how school structures (and those that are in charge of implementing them) lead to students dropping out by following an incoming class of students in a NYC high school (of which, less than a third graduate). This study illuminates that dropping out is not the fault of students, but of those who have systemically framed a dropout school culture.

Hantzopoulos, M. and Tyner-Mullings, A. (eds) (2012). *Critical small schools:* Moving beyond privatization in New York City urban educational reform, Charlotte, NC: Information Age Publishing.

This publication features many empirical case studies about the successes and challenges of the small schools movement in NYC and the likely implications for urban public educational policy. While challenging the concept of charter schools as the panacea for educational reform, the authors discuss how small schools can help narrow the achievement gap and increase graduation and college acceptance rates for historically marginalized youth when certain practices and pedagogies (culturally relevant, social justice oriented, care-based) are implemented in schools.

Valenzuela, A. (1999). *Substractive Schooling: US-Mexican Youth and the Politics of Caring*. Ithaca, NY: SUNY Press.

This classic ethnography shows how schools subtract resources from immigrant youth by dismissing their definition of education and by following assimilationist policies and practices that minimize their culture and language.

References

Advancement Project (2011). *Federal policy, ESEA Re-Authorization and the School to Prison Pipeline*. A joint position paper with Education Law Center, FairTest, The Forum for Education and Democracy, Juvenile Law Center, and the NAACP Legal Defense and Educational Fund, Inc.

American Civil Liberties Union (2010). *ACLU Lawsuit Challenges Abusive Police Practices in New York City Schools*. Retrieved from www.aclu.org on 1 October 2011.

Amrein, A. T. and Berliner, D. C. (2003). The effects of high-stakes testing on student motivation and learning. *Educational Leadership* 60(5): 32–3.

Antorp-Gonzalez, R. (2011). *Schools as Radical Sanctuaries: Decolonizing Urban Education through the Eyes of Youth of Color*. Charlotte, NC: Information Age Publishing.

Antorp-Gonzalez, R. and de Jesús, A. (2005). Toward a theory of critical care in urban small school reform: Examining structures and pedagogies of caring in two Latino community-based schools. *International Journal of Qualitative Studiesin Education* 19(4): 409–33.

Arbuthnot, K. (2011). *Filling in the Blanks: Understanding the Black/White Achievement Gap*. Charlotte, NC: Information Age Publishing.

Bajaj, M. (2009). Why Context Matters: Understanding the Material Conditions of School-Based Caring in Zambia. *International Journal of Qualitative Studies in Education*. 22(4): 379–98.

Bartlett, L. and Koyama, J. (2012). Additive schooling: A critical small school for Latino Youth. In M. Hantzopoulos and A. Tyner-Mullings (eds), *Critical Small Schools: Moving beyond Privatization in New York City Public School Reform*. Charlotte, NC: Information Age Publishing, pp. 79–102.

Bartlett, L. and Garcia, O. (2011). *Additive Schooling in Subtractive Times: Bilingual Education and Dominican Immigrant Youth in the Heights*. Nashville, TN: Vanderbilt University Press.

Bowditch, C. (1993). Getting rid of troublemakers: High school disciplinary procedures and the production of dropouts. *Social Problems* 40: 493–509.

Bridgeland, J., Dilulio, J. and Morrson, K. (2006). *The Silent Epidemic: Perspectives from High School Drop Outs*. Report for Civic Enterprises.

Bridgeland, J., Dilulio, J. and Balfanz, R. (2009). *The High School Dropout Problem: Perspectives of Teachers and Principals*. Retrieved from www.eddigest.com on 7 November 2011.

Christle, C. A., Jolivette, K. and Nelson, C. M. (2007). School characteristics related to high school dropout rates. *Remedial and SpecialEducation* 28: 325–39.

Christle, C. A., Nelson, C. M. and Jolivette, K. (2004). School characteristics related to the use of suspension. *Education and Treatmentof Children* 27: 509–26.

De Jesus, A. (2012). Authentic caring and community driven Reform: The case of El Puente Academy for peace and justice. In M. Hantzopoulos and A. Tyner-Mullings (eds), *Critical Small Schools: Moving beyond Privatization in New York City Public School Reform*. Charlotte, NC: Information Age Publishing, pp. 63–78.

Fergusen, A. (2001). *Bad Boys: Public Schools in the Making of Black Masculinity*. Ann Arbor: University of Michigan Press.

Fine, M. (1991). *Framing Dropouts: Notes on the Politics of an Urban High School*. Albany: State University of New York.

Freire, P. (1972/2003). *The Pedagogy of the Oppressed*. New York: Continuum Press.

Futrell, M. and Rotberg, I. C. (2002) (Oct). Predictable casualties. *Education Week* 22(5): 34–48.

Hantzopoulos, M. (2009). Transformative schooling in restrictive times: The critical small schools movement and standards-based reform in the United States. In F. Vavrus and L. Bartlett (eds), *Comparatively Knowing: Vertical Case Study Research in Comparative and Development Education*. New York: Palgrave, pp. 111–26.

Hantzopoulos, M. (2011a). Deepening democracy: How one school's fairness Committee offers an alternative to "discipline." Reprinted with permission from *Rethinking Schools* in *Schools: Studies in Education* 8(1): 112–16.

Hantzopoulos, M. (2011b). Institutionalizing critical peace education in public schools: A case for comprehensive implementation. *Journal of Peace Education* 8(3): 225–42.

Hantzopoulos, M. (2012a). When cultures collide: Students' successes and challenges as transformative change agents within and beyond a democratic school. In M. Hantzopoulos and A. Tyner-Mullings (eds), *Critical Small Schools: Moving beyond Privatization in New York City Public School Reform*. Charlotte, NC: Information Age Publishing, pp. 189–212.

Hantzopoulos, M. (2012b). Human rights education as public school reform. *Peace Review: A Journal of Social Justice* 24: 36–45.

Hantzopoulos, M. and Tyner-Mullings, A. (2012). Introduction. *Critical small schools:* Moving beyond privatization in New York City public school reform, Charlotte, NC: Information Age Publishing, pp. xxv–xliv.

Hayward, E. (2002, 19 June). Middle school dropout rate up. *Boston Herald*, p. 3.

Horn, C. (2003). High-stakes Testing and Students: Stopping or perpetuating a cycle of failure. *Theory into Practice* 42(1): 30–41.

Karp, S. (2006). Band-aids or bulldozers. *Rethinking Schools* 20(3): 26–9.

Katsyiannis, A., Zhang, D., Ryan, J. and Jones, J. (2007). High stakes testing and students with disabilities: Challenges and promises. *Journal of Disability Policy Studies* 8(3): 160–7.

Lesser, A. Butler-Kisber, L., Fortin, L., Marcitte, D., Potvin, P. and Royer, E. (2008). Shade of disengagement: High school dropouts speak out. *Social Psychology of Education* 11(1): 25–42.

Lee, T., Cornell, D., Gregory, A. and Fan, X. (2011). High suspension schools and dropout rates for Black and White students. *Education and the Treatment of Children* 35: 167–92.

Marchant, G. (2004). What is at stake with high stakes testing? *Ohio Journal of Science* 104(2): 2–7.

Maudau, G. F. and Clarke, M. (2001). The adverse impact of high stakes testing on minority students: Evidence from 100 years of test data. In G. Orfield and M. Kornhaber (eds), Raising standards or raising barriers? Inequality and high stakes testing in public education (pp. 2–49). New York, NY: The Century Foundation.

McNeil, L., Coppola, E., Radigan, J. and Vazquez-Heilig, J. (2011). Avoidable losses: High stakes accountability and the dropout crisis. *Education Policy Archives.* Retrieved from www. *http://epaa.asu.edu/ojs/article/view/28* on 7 November 2012.

Menken, K. (2008). *English Learners Left Behind: Standardized Testing as Language Policy.* Clevedon, Avon: Multilingual Matters.

Mukuria, G. (2002). Disciplinary challenges: How do principals address this dilemma. *Urban Education* 37(3): 432–52.

National Economic and Social Rights Initiative (2007). *Deprived of Dignity: Degrading Treatment and Abusive Discipline in New York City & Los Angeles Public Schools.* New York: NESRI.

New York Civil Liberties Union (2009). *Safety with Dignity: Alternatives to the Over-Policing of Schools.* A joint report with Make the Road and the Annenberg Institute of School Reform. New York: NYCLU.

Raffaele-Mendez, L., Knoff, H. M. and Ferron, J. M. (2002). School demographic variables and out-of-school suspension rates: A quantitative and qualitative analysis of a large, ethnically diverse school district. *Psychology in the Schools* 39(3): 259–77.

Rivera-McCuthcen, R. (2012). Considering Context: Exploring a Small Schools Struggle to Maintain Its Educational Vision. In M. Hantzopoulos and A. Tyner-Mullings (eds), *Critical Small Schools: Moving beyond Privatization in New York City Public School Reform.* Charlotte, NC: Information Age Publishing, pp. 21–39.

Rodriguez, L. (2010). What schools can do about the dropout crisis. *Leadership* 40: 18–22.

Rodriguez, L. and Conchas, G. (2008). *Small Schools and Urban Youth: Using the Power of School Culture to Engage Students.* Thousand Oaks, CA: Sage Press.

Rumberger, R. (2004). Why students drop out of school. In G Orfield (ed.), *Dropouts in America: Confronting the Crisis.* Cambridge, MA: Harvard University Press, pp. 131–55.

Shiller, J. (2012). City Prep: A Culture of Care in an Era of Data Driven Reform. In M. Hantzopoulos and A. Tyner-Mullings (eds), *Critical Small Schools: Moving beyond Privatization in New York City Public School Reform.* Charlotte, NC: Information Age Publishing, pp. 3–20.

Suh, S. and Suh, J. (2007). Risk factors and levels of risk for high school dropouts. *Professional School Counseling* 10: 297–306.

Tyner-Mullings, A. (2012). Redefining Success: How CPESS Students Reached The Goals That Mattered. In M. Hantzopoulos and A. Tyner-Mullings (eds), *Critical Small Schools: Moving beyond Privatization in New York City Public School Reform.* Charlotte, NC: Information Age Publishing, pp. 137–65.

Valenzuela, A. (1999). *Substractive Schooling: US–Mexican Youth and the Politics of Caring.* Ithaca, NY: SUNY Press.

Vasquez-Heilig, J. and Darling-Hammond, L. (2008). Accountability Texas-style: The progress and learning of urban minority students in a high-stakes testing context. *Educational Evaluation and Policy Analysis* 30(2): 75–110.

Schooling for Youth and Community Empowerment and Resilience During and After Violent Conflict

2

Zeena Zakharia

Chapter Outline

Introduction

Over the past 15 years, more than 35 countries have experienced armed conflict, impacting millions of children, with over 40 per cent of the world's out-of-school children living in conflict-affected countries (UNESCO, 2011). In addition, at least 43 million people between 1999 and 2008 were reported to have been displaced by violent conflict. The 2011 Global Monitoring Report on Education for All (EFA) sought to draw attention to the impact of armed conflict on education, asserting a "hidden crisis" for reaching fundamental targets toward educating all of the world's children.

Viewed as a vital conduit for promoting empowerment and other development benefits, education is widely acknowledged as a means by which economically and socially marginalized children and young people can improve the circumstances of their material poverty. Education can also offer a route through which politically marginalized groups might engage in meaningful participation as members of a collective, whether as citizens or noncitizens. Thus, education can serve as a powerful tool to address issues of structural violence, that is, systemic social injustice that manifests itself as inequality, including unequal power over, or participation in, decision-making processes and resource distribution, and "consequently as unequal life chances" (Galtung, 1969, p. 171).[1]

In the context of armed conflict, education also has the potential to mitigate the impact of direct physical violence. By providing support for social and emotional resilience, schools can engage students cognitively, socially, and emotionally to withstand and recover from the physical and psychosocial risks and consequences of war. Schools can also offer students the opportunity to envision and plan for a different future.[2]

This chapter explores schooling for youth and community empowerment and resilience during and after periods of acute violent conflict. Drawing on extensive ethnographic data from a Shi`i Islamic school[3] in Lebanon after the 2006 July war between Hizbullah and Israel,[4] the chapter considers how one school addressed both direct and structural forms of violence within a school whose community was directly impacted by the violence. Whereas literature on education in emergencies focuses largely on the interventions of international organizations to address issues of educational access, literacy development, child protection, and psychosocial well-being (e.g., GCPEA, n.d.; Mundy and Dryden-Peterson, 2011; UNESCO, 2010), this ethnographic study highlights the efforts of a community-centered and community-led school. In particular, this chapter examines the school's approach to educating children and youth who, at the time of the study, were marginalized by war and displacement, and by a history of collective structural violence. In exploring some of the pedagogical practices and features of the school, the chapter goes beyond issues of educational access to consider how a community-centered education, in the context of conflict, might integrate academic, social, and emotional needs to meaningfully address both direct and structural forms of violence. In doing so, this particular school promotes the empowerment and resilience of youth and their community, suggesting elements of a framework for what I call a dynamic community empowerment model of schooling. Through this form of schooling, students and teachers are engaged as agents in personal and community development, both as individuals and as a collective. The chapter concludes by drawing out some of these elements for further consideration.

Violent conflict in Lebanon and the marginalization of the Shi`a

Lebanon's long history of civil strife is inextricably linked to a broader history of regional, cross-border, national, and localized armed conflicts. Some of these conflicts predate the state, while others are more recent. External regional tensions, combined with internal tensions and disparities, have contributed to violent conflicts throughout the past six decades. These have been significantly influenced by regional dynamics, including Lebanon's central position within the Arab–Israeli conflict and protracted Israeli (1978–2000) and Syrian (1976–2005) occupations. The legacies of war, occupation, displacement, and structural violence continue to be felt by the Lebanese, Palestinians, Armenians, Kurds, and more recently, Iraqis and Syrians, as well as by other peoples who have made Lebanon their permanent or temporary home (Zakharia, 2011).

Sectarianism, or "the deployment of religious heritage as a primary marker of modern political identity" (Makdisi, 2000, p. 7), has underpinned the mobilization for major episodes of armed conflict in Lebanon over the last century. Reinforced by colonial governance mechanisms and missionary activities, sectarianism first took root under nineteenth-century Ottoman rule, when it emerged both as a political discourse and as a bureaucratic practice (Makdisi, 2000), in which diverse religious minorities were differentially governed on the basis of their sect. This gradual process of sectarian development in political and social life was consolidated under French colonial rule (1920–1943), which groomed a Christian political elite and forged the sect-based political system of the newly formed Lebanese state in 1943 (Zakharia, 2011). The confessional power-sharing formula, or government representation based on religious sect, inadequately represented particular groups, and thereby, their access to power and resources. These structural inequalities led to growing unrest, in part fuelling the Lebanese civil war of 1975–1990. During the war, it is estimated that 150,000–200,000 people were killed, more than 100,000 were severely wounded, and approximately 17,000 disappeared and remain unaccounted for. An estimated 810,000 people were displaced (UNDP, 1997), of which a quarter emigrated permanently. While scholars and political analysts have attributed multiple, complex factors to fueling the civil war—including an unjust confessional political system, grievances over unequal distributions of power and resources, developments in the Arab–Israeli conflict, and evolving international and regional interests (Khalaf, 2002; Tueni, 1990)—sectarianism, not as primordial identity, but as social and political practice, emerges from these explanations as a core driver of conflict.

In fact, sectarianism has come to pervade societal institutions in the post-civil war period (Khalaf, 2002), whereby constitutional and administrative reforms failed to address the core drivers of conflict. Rather, they appear to have reinscribed sectarianism, exacerbating various forms of structural violence through systems of inequitable access to resources and development. For example, public expenditure in the areas of education, health, and infrastructure has been allocated by sect on a per capita basis (Salti and Chaaban, 2010). This means that public services have not been provided equitably, or on the basis of need. As a result, internal regional disparities and class–income inequalities have widened since the end of the civil war (UNDP, 2007).

Inequitable development in education has been just one manifestation of these inequalities. For the Shi`a at the focus of this study, such inequalities in education date back to the earliest emergence of schools in Lebanon. By the early-1800s, European and American colonial powers with competing interests in the Ottoman-controlled region of Lebanon had begun to establish Christian missionary schools for their particular religious communities. Influenced by the success of this endeavor, the Sunni Muslim Ottoman authority also opened schools, based on the French-Catholic model, but with Islamic features (Fortna, 2002). Shi`i Muslims, however, were excluded from the educational developments of this period (Abouchedid and Nassar, 2000). Under Sunni Ottoman rule, they were often persecuted, and their material and educational development were ignored by colonial and missionary enterprises. At independence from the French colonial mandate in 1943, the confessional, or sect-based, political system perpetuated the underrepresentation of the Shi`a in government, and later in post-independence development. This system institutionalized sectarianism as a means for accessing resources, thus neglecting the development needs of the Shi`a in the post-independence and post-civil war periods. This unequal development and collective deprivation eventually contributed to the mobilization of the Shi`a into various political parties in the 1960s and 1970s, and later into sectarian political movements (Deeb, 2006).

Today, Shi`i Muslims in Lebanon comprise one of 18 officially recognized religious sects. As a population that has been historically marginalized politically, economically, and socially, their educational movement is more recent, with the first Shi`a-run school founded in Beirut in 1929. Additional formal schools did not appear until the latter half of the century. In particular, the Shi`a-run private school movement gathered intensity only in the early 1990s, after the end of the civil war.

Thus, a history of inequitable development, including in education, served to disadvantage the Shi`a community and its youth, from before the formation of the nation-state through to post-civil war reforms. The inequitable, sect-based disbursement of public funds and services during the post-civil war period resulted in certain regions, such as South Lebanon and the Bekaa Valley, being underserved. The Shi`a constitute a large proportion of these regions' populations. Their marginalization has led to large migrations to Beirut and its suburbs, where access to schools and services is more prevalent. These dynamics have been compounded by the positioning of Lebanon within the Arab–Israeli conflict. Israeli withdrawal from South Lebanon and the Bekaa Valley, from where many of the focal school's community hail, left behind 430,000 unexploded ordinances (UXOs) in these regions. These have claimed 27 lives and injured 232, many of them children and young people (Zakharia, 2011). UXOs have also limited agricultural development, perpetuating economic hardship and sustained insecurity for regions in which the Shi`a reside. In addition, Syria's influence in Lebanon and current civil turmoil continue to impact localized conflicts in Lebanon.

Schooling and armed conflict

Schools are very often objects of attack in armed conflicts. Attacks on schools include direct targeting that causes destruction to school buildings, or otherwise compromises their operations through occupation, shelling, propaganda, and harm to physical infrastructure or personnel (UN, 2010). In the Middle East, this has been particularly true; in the context of Iraq, the occupied Palestinian territory, and Lebanon, schools have been repeatedly targeted in military operations (see O'Malley, 2010, for an extended discussion). Furthermore, with the recent Arab uprisings, education has been impacted by violence in a number of countries across the region, including Bahrain, Egypt, Libya, Syria, Tunisia, and Yemen.

Whether explicitly targeted or not, educational provision is significantly disrupted by violent conflict through the creation of physical obstacles to reaching school and the physical or psychosocial harm caused to students, their teachers, and families (Zakharia, 2004). Armed conflict negatively impacts the learning environment. Further, the physical and psychological threat posed by armed conflict creates new vulnerabilities for children and young people, particularly for those from historically marginalized communities. In turn, these young people are doubly disadvantaged, both by their historical context and the contemporary realities of war. Armed conflict also disrupts essential social services and protective environments that "empower adolescents and young people to forge their own lives" (Pybus and Jacoby, 2011, p. 41). Thus, by denying children and young people social services such as education, armed conflict not only impacts them through direct violence, but also perpetuates or creates new forms of structural violence.

In Lebanon, the civil war had a devastating impact on formal schooling, effectively crippling the public education system, while contributing to a proliferation of private schools. Parents increasingly enrolled their children in private and parochial schools near home, in part because of the perception that these schools were better managed, and also because of the immobility caused by the security situation, which prevented students from reaching schools in other neighborhoods. Public high schools, in particular, were chaotic during this period (Assal and Farrel, 1992) due to the presence of arms and the recruitment of young people from schools into armed militias. The civil war, with its sectarian underpinnings, also buttressed the development of confessional schools, which in turn, endorsed the divisive features of schooling.

Thus, as a consequence of both a history of missionary activity and armed conflict in the modern period, the Lebanese educational system today is comprised of a diversity of schools, of which the majority is private and parochial. The Lebanese Constitution allows for confessional groups, or religious sects, to organize their own schools. However, all schools are expected to follow a centralized national curriculum, regulated by the Ministry of Education and Higher Education (MEHE). Post-civil war educational reforms, however, failed to institute a national history curriculum, leaving confessional schools to deliver their own versions of history. Thus, a divisive civil war discourse continues to be reproduced among a population of students who were born years after the civil war (Larkin, 2010).

The 2006 July war between Hizbullah and Israel, and the internal political violence that followed, produced new challenges for young people and their schools. These events set the context for the current study. The 34-day war killed 1,187 civilians as well as combatants, and injured another 4,398. One million people were displaced, out of which 600,000 were sheltered by host families or in public buildings, such as schools (Kelly and White, 2006). The war devastated civilian infrastructure, including 342 schools, with an estimated 45 million USD in war damages to education (Zakharia, 2011). These schools were disproportionately Shi`i educational institutions. Further, approximately 1.2 million UXOs were dropped, impacting areas largely populated by Shi`i Muslims in South Lebanon, the Bekaa Valley, and Beirut's southern suburbs.

The 2006–2007 academic year that followed was characterized by postwar recovery and reconstruction, as well as by new internal political violence and upheaval. An environment of insecurity prevailed due to a series of politically motivated assassinations, violent protests, and roadside bombs detonated in civilian areas. These caused daily disruptions to schooling. Furthermore, in 2007, the Nahr el-Bared crisis, which involved a war between the Lebanese Army and an al-Qaeda-inspired insurgent militia, resulted in the destruction of a major Palestinian refugee camp and its surroundings in North Lebanon, displacing thousands of students and their families. At the same time, internal sectarian violence flared up amidst a power vacuum and deepening polarization between pro-government and opposition parties and their allies.

This period of violence and upheaval was particularly poignant for the students and teachers at the Shi`i school discussed in this chapter. Many students and teachers lost friends or family members during the 2006 July war, and the school took in a number of orphans. In addition, many were internally displaced and lived in temporary housing following the destruction of their homes.

Political and faith-based organizations played a significant role in reconstruction and recovery after the 2006 July war and the 2007 Nahr el-Bared crisis and have been credited with the resilience of the education sector in Lebanon (Euro-Trends, 2009). Thus, while the confessional orientation of schooling has both reflected and promoted social divisions, it also appears to have contributed significantly to the resilience of schools and their communities, who have made extraordinary efforts to maintain the functioning of their schools under difficult circumstances. This study considers one such school, its youth, and community.

Data collection

This chapter considers how one school addressed both direct and structural forms of violence, thus contributing to youth and community empowerment and resilience for students from a historically marginalized community in the context of armed conflict and sustained insecurity. The research presented here draws on a larger study comprising 21 months of fieldwork between 2005 and 2007 at 10 religious and secular Lebanese secondary schools in the Greater Beirut region during one of the most violent periods in recent years. This chapter makes particular use of qualitative data collected during the 2006–2007 academic year through daily participant observation at the Shi`i focal school. The data were collected during class time, library activities, and extracurricular undertakings, such as performances, lectures, and exhibits at the school. In addition, data were drawn from interviews with teachers, students, and administrators; conversations with parents; and school documents.

It was in the classrooms that my attention was first drawn to the content and form of education at this school. My initial purpose was to study language policy, and from this inquiry, emerged a world of schooling immersed in transformative learning. Not only did teachers work with students to critically analyze issues of significance to peace and human rights, but they also taught in ways that invited critical reflection, creative undertakings, and a reconsideration of values. In particular, critical reflection was a central tenet that involved rational and emotional considerations, reflecting on the self, the community, and the other, while recognizing differences. I began to sit in hallways and the library to witness these undertakings in alternative spaces. I observed extracurricular activities, community events, and social action projects. I read the materials on the walls, which consistently bore new student projects, undertaken through collaborative group work. Through these daily interactions,

I came to observe the multiple ways in which teachers and students together contended with direct and structural violence, both in and out of the class, in turn, negotiating individual and community empowerment and resilience.

A community centered school

The Shi`i school at the focus of this study was first established as a girls' school in 1997 and later grew to include boys in gender-segregated classrooms. At the time of the study, it enrolled over 2,500 Shi`i students in grades K to 12 and followed the Lebanese national curriculum in Arabic, English, and French, geared toward the national examinations at grades 9 (Brevet) and 12 (Baccalaureate). It was a trilingual university preparatory school.

The school was run by an explicit faith-based organization and mission, by and for the Shi`a community. While the school was open to all students and teachers, its spiritual and school leadership, instructional and support staff, and attendant population self-identified as Shi`a. As part of its religious mission, the school held bi-weekly religion classes and daily morning prayers.

As a community-centered institution, the Shi`i school both taught the national curriculum and engaged students in community-centered issues as part of its vision for personal and community empowerment and development. Teachers and administrators served as role models; they came from the community and were also engaged in their own learning and professional development, as well as in the development of the community through a variety of community outreach and educational efforts. Students and teachers came from varied socioeconomic backgrounds. They mostly lived in the largely less affluent southern suburb of Beirut, which was directly targeted during the 2006 July war.

The focal school viewed itself as a school that was engaged in a struggle for community development, as expressed in school literature and by teachers and administrators. The notion of development, or progress, commonly articulated among teachers, administrators, and parents included both material and spiritual progress. This vision of progress included an element of individual and community empowerment emerging from intellectual progress, achieved through a process of inquiry and critical reflection. Such notions reflected the teachings of the school and the community's spiritual leader.[5] Such discourse was also prevalent in the largely Shi`a-inhabited neighborhood in which the school was situated (Deeb, 2006).

According to one Arabic teacher, parents sent their children to the school because it was inclusive and educated the "whole child," including intellectual, social, and spiritual aspects. She explained:

> It is open to all. We work on the students' personality and conduct activities that build on a number of areas of personal development, including religious. We are always moving forward and experimenting to make progress. This makes us enjoy a good reputation (Interview in Arabic, 3 May 2007).

Indeed, the school had many of the features that education scholars and practitioners would identify with a "good school." The school had qualified teachers, specialized support staff, a team of social workers, and a clinic. It had a physical environment tailored for a range of educational activities, flexible classrooms fit for collaborative learning, student work on display, and a solid investment in a multipurpose library. According to the principal, the library was "an authority in the school [where] everyone knows the importance of the library and developing research skills" (Interview in English, 17 April 2007). In addition, students performed well on the national examinations, and teachers and staff were engaged in ongoing professional development, evaluation, and research of their own and in collaboration with other scholars. The institution itself also conducted research on its own progress and community needs in order to develop evidence-based programming for its students.

Contending with direct violence

The administration, teachers, and support staff at the Shi`i school employed a number of strategies to contend with direct violence and to mitigate the effects of direct violence on the community. These efforts took place in the classroom as part of curricular content and also beyond as part of extracurricular activities, engaging both students and the larger community. Rather than ignoring the presence of political violence or armed conflict during classroom teaching, or stopping academic work to attend to the psychosocial needs of the students, teachers integrated these concerns across the curriculum and extracurricular programs. Their attention to direct violence was evident in (1) instructional content, both academic and extracurricular, (2) instructional form, or pedagogical strategies, (3) student skill development, or skill areas taught, and (4) educational support structures. I discuss each of these below.

One illustration of how direct violence was engaged through academic content and form involved a writing project for elementary school French classes at the start of the 2006–2007 academic year. During the summer war of the previous months, images by Associated Press photographer Sebastian Scheiner had been widely circulated in the media and over the internet. The images, taken at a heavy artillery position in northern Israel, show Israeli girls writing messages, presumably to their Lebanese counterparts, on shells similar to those launched into southern Lebanese villages.[6] Students, who were learning French as a second language, were asked to write letters in French in response to the Israeli children in these images. According to the French language coordinator:

> At first we let them free-write whatever they wanted or needed to say. After the free-write, we examined the letters, which, as you can imagine, were . . . terrible, as a first reaction. We then engaged students in a conversation about their responses (Interview in Arabic, 10 May 2007).

During the discussion and the reflection process that followed, teachers and students talked about their feelings and drew on religious understanding to develop their ideas about violence: "We discussed how Islam and Judaism are above this and do not allow for this kind of response," referring to student expressions of retaliation or bad will (Interview in Arabic, 10 May 2007). Teachers then had the students rewrite their letters. According to the French language coordinator, these new letters were more thoughtful, reflecting greater understanding and a processing of emotions, such as sadness, hatred, and fear. Thus, through the writing, discussion, and reflection process, teachers addressed the psychosocial impact of the 2006 July war on their particular community, while meeting the academic writing goals of the national curriculum for French language acquisition. In other words, they employed the writing curriculum as a "vehicle for trauma intervention" (Teacher interview in Arabic, 10 May 2007) and as an opportunity for students to reflect critically on their attitudes toward violence.

It was not only in this particular writing project that teachers addressed the impact of direct violence; it was also in other lessons, through a variety of research, writing, and performance projects. In each of these instances, teachers attended to social and emotional needs, such as fears of resumed hostilities, while bringing these concerns into the academic process. In this way, across the curriculum, they engaged the students in thinking about militarism, terrorism, human rights violations, and other forms of direct violence that were impacting their community.

Students also produced books, plays, and artwork about the summer war. Such pedagogical approaches engaged students with art therapeutically to develop their sense of hope and resilience. For example, primary grade students collaboratively produced a large collage that involved about 60 small photographs of buildings devastated during the summer war. This project demonstrates one of the ways in which teachers addressed the impact of direct violence in extracurricular content. First, the photographs were glued to a large poster board. Next, images of flowers, butterflies, suns, houses, and people were painted over the photographs, using thick, bright brushstrokes. Depicting community resilience, the multicolored images were superimposed on the photographs of physical destruction. The collage was exhibited at the spring art and book fair, which was visited by family and community members.

The school also contended with direct violence through the development of relevant skills in and out of class. For example, the school addressed survival skills, including landmine education and coping skills, such as what to do when faced with various situations in the context of war. Illustrated pamphlets containing this information were also distributed to families. Using little text, these pamphlets were devised to be accessible to children and adults with various levels of literacy.

Finally, the school sought to mitigate the effects of direct violence and to contribute to the resilience of students and community members through a number of educational support structures. The school had full-time social workers and conducted community outreach programs to support children and their families. The social workers worked with specific age groups and their families. Their charge was to ensure that children and youth requiring academic or psychosocial supports were referred to developmentally appropriate counseling, specialized educational plans, and other forms of care. In addition, the school provided support to students who were orphaned by the conflict, educating them for free and providing academic and psychosocial supports. Thus, by addressing the impact of direct violence through classroom activities, extracurricular programming, and educational support structures, the Shi`i school sought to address the cognitive, social, and emotional needs of students and their families. In doing so, they addressed youth and community resilience, both individually and relationally, that is, as members of a community impacted by violence.

Contending with structural violence

The school addressed structural violence through an infused social justice curriculum that attended to various forms of oppression related to gender, race/ethnicity, poverty, religious belief, political freedom, nationality and citizenship status, among other things. Teachers and students also engaged with economic, social, and political rights through instructional content, critical and participatory pedagogy, and through events and celebrations. Furthermore, the school focused on skill development related to cross-cultural communication, community activism, and leadership. As with direct violence, engagement with structural violence was evident in aspects of the school's (1) instructional content, (2) instructional form, (3) skill development, and (4) the educational support structures extended to students, their families, and the wider community, as part of a community-centered empowerment and development effort. In this section, I provide illustrative examples of some of these strategies.

Gendered relations—an important aspect of conflict sensitivity in educational programming—were a common theme across the secondary school-level girls' activities. In one lesson, Grade 10 girls explored male–female relations through an activity in which students negotiated differing views within the class community about their relationships with their male counterparts. The teacher drew on students' experiences with friendship and marital engagement as the instructional content or "text" for analysis. She encouraged critical reflection on different ways of establishing relationships with men. Through the discussion, the teacher established a norm for the empowered partner, one who develops her autonomous power while developing interdependence with another person (Field Notes, 29 May 2007).

Other lessons engaged students in research about the role of women in public service and political office. Such projects included interviewing high profile women in Lebanon. Projects displayed on classroom walls and in hallways depicted discussion on the balance between work and home life and the impact of conflict on women's lives. In this way, girls critically reflected on their roles within their families, community, and professional spheres. Through a guided process of critical reflection and inquiry, they considered the constraints that had been placed on their gender and how these might be renegotiated in tandem with their values.

Research was a key component of the school's ethic and an important aspect of both instructional form and skill development. Research served as a tool for inquiry and for the interrogation of structural violence, such as institutionalized forms of discrimination. It also served to gather evidence in order to critically reflect on a position, or widely held belief, including contested histories that have led to conflict or persecution. Thus, students and teachers actively engaged in learning and using tools for inquiry across the curriculum, including qualitative and quantitative research methods, such as developing surveys and conducting interviews. They also used basic technologies to conduct research, to present findings, and to make documentary and narrative films. Students of all ages also wrote books and displayed them on tables at the annual book fair, alongside publishers who were invited to promote books by their publishing houses. The students learned public speaking skills and actually presented with the support of multimedia presentations at large public gatherings, such as at a UNESCO-sponsored "Education for All" event that served as the culmination of the school's Human Rights Week.

The "Education for All" event promoted education as a fundamental right that has not been equally enjoyed across countries of the Middle East. The celebration provides an illustrative example of the dynamic ways in which the school engaged with structural violence, both in and out of the class, and as part of community outreach. It took place at a community-based venue in order to welcome hundreds of guests from the community. It not only showcased the students' research, thinking, and artwork on the subject of human rights—education as a right, in particular—but also served as an educational forum for the community. Secondary students presented regional statistics on education and described some of the obstacles to achieving Education for All in Arab countries. Children, young and old, inspired the adults to return to school through skits and songs, in which information on literacy classes for parents was provided. In addition, decorated bulletin boards pictured teachers' professional training courses on the right to education, depicting teachers as ongoing learners. In this way, the event provided a venue for promoting learning for all members of the school community, as part of a commitment to community empowerment and development.

In the classroom, teachers engaged students in collaborative group work and critical participatory dialogue. By drawing on students' experiences and narratives to construct the class texts, teachers encouraged students to negotiate their positions, or beliefs, in dialogue with others, and based on research evidence, as well as on their own thinking and feelings. Through this process, students were encouraged to question oppressive patterns of social, political, and economic organization in relation to the collective struggles of diverse peoples, such as the Palestinians, Native Americans, African Americans, migrants, and laborers, as well as in relation to their own experiences of gender, class, religion, disability, race, and citizenship status. They were then encouraged to link this learning to specific community-centered social action projects. In this way, students also worked toward greater justice and understanding of their struggle as social agents and in tandem with others in their community and around the world.

For example, in one Arabic lesson, secondary school girls engaged in a book talk led by a student at the school library. The student introduced the book's author as a communist, "when proclaiming communist beliefs was illegal in the Arab world." She explained that the author was imprisoned and tortured for his beliefs, which he eventually rescinded by signing a statement to end his suffering (Field Notes, 2 June 2007).[7] She then led an animated discussion that touched upon the issue of political imprisonment, the significance of political and religious freedoms for the well-being of civil society, and the principles of democracy, particularly within the context of the largely nondemocratic countries of the Middle East. The Arabic teacher and librarian helped guide the discussion, saying:

> We have to understand that just as we have our beliefs and ideas and opinions, others have theirs and we must accept their right to have them and voice them. And from an Islamic point of view too—to accept the Other and the Other's point of view. We cannot dream of a real civil society otherwise (Field Notes, 2 June 2007).

This student-led lesson addressed structural violence in both content and form, allowing students to learn from their peers, to reflect on the constraints that have been placed on their own beliefs as a historically persecuted religious minority, and to consider how they might ensure the rights of others. Significantly, this form of learning assisted students in envisioning a world in which their own rights were included as part of a democratic society. By conducting this and other critical dialogues in Modern Standard Arabic, English, and French, students also developed language skills to engage in such conversations with a wider community. According to an academic coordinator, developing multiple language skills was part of the school's vision for community development and progress, which entailed students developing their abilities as public speakers and in communication across cultures (Interview in Arabic, 12 June 2007).

In short, the school addressed the issue of structural violence with children and youth, not only as an object of study, but also through the transformative process of individual and collective empowerment. The school also prepared students for leadership, activism, and service to the community and to the nation. Through various educational support structures, including community outreach for literacy education and various social service initiatives, the school further engaged students individually and relationally with their communities in addressing structural violence.

Youth and community empowerment and resilience: An integrated approach

The school activities described in the previous sections suggest four dimensions of an integrated approach to youth and community empowerment and resilience. First, the school's practices concurrently addressed social, emotional, and cognitive needs. For example, lessons met academic goals while attending to the social and emotional concerns of students, such as the fear of resumed violence. By attending to the psychosocial impact of direct violence, and thus the concerns that were distracting the students, teachers and learners were also able to advance academic engagement. Consequently, by meeting (or surpassing) national curricular standards, the school demonstrated a commitment to addressing educational inequalities as a form of structural violence.

The school's practices also demonstrated an integrated approach to youth and community empowerment and resilience by concomitantly addressing direct and structural violence. In integrating these aspects, the school attended to both the negative impacts of conflict, as well as to transformative processes toward greater social justice and democratic engagement.

The third dimension of an integrated approach, as suggested by the school's practices, is the holistic engagement of instructional content, form, skill development, and educational support structures, toward youth and community empowerment and resilience. Through academic and extracurricular activities and service provision, the school was able to work on aspects of both direct and structural violence through an infused curriculum, while also addressing educational standards and preparing students for national examinations.

Significantly, the school considered the individual and the community relationally, whereby students and teachers were involved in a struggle for intellectual, material, and spiritual development, concurrently as individuals and as an interdependent collective. Within this community-centered model, the content and form of education, including research and social action, are embedded in local struggles, and schooling emerges as a political project, committed to youth and community empowerment and resilience. Educational structures supported multiple school actors in this process, including teachers as learners with ongoing professional development. It aimed to advance their knowledge of instructional content, pedagogical form, and skill development in areas such as human rights education training and skills to contend with the impact of direct violence on their students, their own families, and the community. Furthermore, the school itself was engaged in learning by conducting research on its programs and community needs. By holding performances and events, disseminating materials, and engaging in other forms of community outreach with students, the school extended this learning to the community, addressing student and community empowerment and resilience interdependently. Such approaches embed the students in a community of learners, encouraging personal progress as part of a larger bid toward community development.

Importantly, as a community-centered model of schooling, the content of education reflected the values and aspirations of an internally diverse community. This was possible because teachers had a good understanding of their students and the varied social circumstances and political orientations of their families. This helped them to navigate classroom discussions on sensitive social and political issues and to advance students' learning in a democratic learning space.

As we have seen, four dimensions of integration characterize the school's approach to youth and community empowerment and resilience (see summary Table 2.1 below). These dimensions suggest that the school would be better described as having a dynamic community empowerment model of schooling. I take up this notion in the concluding section.

Table 2.1 Four dimensions of an integrated approach to youth and community empowerment and resilience

1. Integrates social, emotional, and cognitive needs
2. Integrates direct and structural violence
3. Integrates instructional content, form, skill development, and educational support structures
4. Integrates individual and community issues

Conclusion: Contextualizing a dynamic community empowerment model of schooling

This chapter considered how one school, through a community-centered model of schooling, addressed both direct and structural forms of violence for a historically marginalized community, thus contributing to youth and community empowerment and resilience in the context of political violence and sustained insecurity. As a dynamic community empowerment model of schooling, the Shi`i school worked concurrently on empowering the individual and the community, thus developing the agency of both relationally. Education within a dynamic community empowerment model is not limited to issues of significance to community membership; that is, it is not insular, as might be suggested by the notion of "community-centered." Rather, at the same time that the school is community-centered in aspects of its instructional content, form, skill development and support structures, it also supports students from a disadvantaged community to prepare for their active roles in a democratic society. In that sense, it is dynamic. In other words, it is inward- and outward-looking; past- and forward-looking; resisting the "marginal" status of the community; engaging students as learners, teachers, and community activists; and educating parents and community in order to support students as empowered agents.

Addressing direct and structural forms of violence is a social process that requires contextualized knowledge of the community. While this chapter focused on a particular period in which violent political conflict was salient in the everyday lives of the school community, it is important to remember that various forms of violence preceded and succeeded this time period, requiring a more complex and long-range view of conflict, empowerment, and resilience. This entails going beyond the security concerns of protection and service delivery, as prioritized by international organizations (Novelli and Smith, 2011). Rather, such concerns must be contextualized and integrated with aspects of education that address structural forms of violence. Further, this chapter suggests that a more integrated approach to youth and community empowerment and resilience is possible and particularly productive through a community-centered education, whereby contextualized educational strategies have matured within a particular sociopolitical context and history.

This contextualization of strategies is central to the competence of this particular school in addressing direct and structural forms of violence.

While a dynamic community empowerment model of schooling holds great promise for peace building, it is important to note that other intervening factors constrain the actions of school actors, and ultimately, the futures of children and young people who have been affected by war and structural violence. Still, this case study suggests that an integrated approach to youth and community empowerment and resilience that is contextualized through localized knowledge, research, activism, and leadership has the potential to transform historically marginalized communities, while preparing young people for democratic engagement within the larger society.

Questions for reflection

1. Have you observed direct and/or structural violence in your own school community? In society? If so, how did your school or other actors seek to address the various forms of violence, if at all?
2. Brainstorm possible approaches or strategies for dealing with direct and structural violence within a school community. Create a table in which you categorize these. In one column, write down the strategies for addressing direct violence and in a second, the strategies for addressing structural violence. Sub-divide the various strategy areas into instructional content, instructional form, skill development, and school support structures, as follows:

Strategy area	**Type of violence**	
	Direct violence	**Structural violence**
Instructional content		
Instructional form		
Skill development		
School structures		

3. The practices of the school described in this chapter suggest four dimensions of an integrated approach to youth and community empowerment and resilience. What do empowerment and resilience mean to you? Why, in your view, might integrated approaches be particularly suitable for addressing these?
4. What aspects of a school make it community-centered? Why might community-centered schools be particularly effective in working with children and young people affected by direct and structural violence? What might be the possible drawbacks to a community-centered approach in the context of armed conflict?

Acknowledgment

I am grateful to Frédérique Weyer, Kimberly Foulds, Arshad Ali, and Maria Hantzopoulos, who provided important input on the development of this chapter. I am also grateful to students, teachers, and administrators at the Shi`i school, who gave me their time and shared with me their strategies and concerns.

Notes

1 Galtung (1969) further describes structural violence as indirect violence that is built into the structure, and thus, unlike direct physical violence, it has no concrete, visible actor or perpetrator. For example, the material poverty of particular groups is a manifestation of structural violence.

2 As Bush and Saltarelli (2000) have explained, education has "two faces" in the context of violent conflict (see also Smith and Vaux, 2003). It can be a driver of conflict, through for example, the divisive, discriminatory, or inadequate portrayal of particular groups and their histories in curricula; or through inequitable structures in schooling. It can also be a driver of peace by addressing structural violence or the root causes of conflict in society. Thus, schooling can serve as a resource for youth and community empowerment and resilience in the context of violent conflict. While the Lebanese educational system is characterized by both of these "faces," this chapter focuses on the potential for positive impacts on children and young people in the context of armed conflict and political violence.

3 To more closely reflect Arabic pronunciation and usage, I use "Shi`i" (adjective) and "Shi`a" (plural noun) in referring to Shiite Muslims or institutions. I use the term "Shi`i school" to refer to the study's focal school.

4 The 2006 summer war is referred to as the "July war" in Lebanon and the "Second Lebanon War" in Israel.

5 The spiritual leadership of the school played a significant role in guiding its educational principles, including reformist ideas about religion and gender, encouraging, for example, spiritual development through inquiry and interpretation, and the active engagement of women and girls in their community. While central to the establishment, development, and guidance of this school, the spiritual leader and the school's hand-picked principal are not discussed in this analysis, in part to protect the confidentiality of participants in line with Institutional Review Board protocol.

6 See Sebastian Scheiner's photography at http://www.apimages.com. Caption: "Israeli girls write messages on a shell at a heavy artillery position near Kiryat Shmona, in northern Israel, next to the Lebanese border, Monday, 17 July 2006."

7 Communism in Lebanon, and other parts of the Arab world, brought together secular intellectuals and multi-faith peoples under its banner, including many Shi`a.

Further reading

Bush, K. and Saltarelli, D. (eds) (2000). *The Two Faces of Education in Ethnic Conflict: Towards a Peacebuilding Education for Children*. Florence: UNICEF Innocenti Insight.

This foundational text provides a useful overview of the ways by which education has been used in the context of conflict to produce both negative and positive impacts on the lives of children.

Machel, G. (2001). *The Impact of War on Children*. London: UNICEF.

This book is an extension of Machel's groundbreaking 1996 United Nations report, entitled "Impact of Armed Conflict on Children" (available at: http://www.unicef.org/graca/). It documents the devastating effects of war on children, drawing on cases from around the world, and is considered the landmark text in drawing global attention to these issues.

Mundy, K. and Dryden-Peterson, S. (eds) (2011). *Educating Children in Conflict Zones: Research, Policy, and Practice for Systemic Change—A Tribute to Jackie Kirk*. New York and London: Teachers College Press.

This collection of case studies examines the educational needs of children impacted by violent conflict and the practical challenges to improving access to, and delivery of, quality education in a number of country contexts.

Winthrop, R. and Kirk, J. (2008). "Learning for a bright future: Schooling, armed conflict, and children's wellbeing." *Comparative Education Review* 52(4): 639–61.

This article draws on research with primary school students from several conflict-affected country contexts to present the various ways by which children conceptualize their own well-being in relation to schooling. The authors argue that, under certain conditions, education can promote children's well-being in the context of armed conflict.

References

Abouchedid, K. and Nassar, R. (2000). "The state of history teaching in private-run confessional schools in Lebanon: Implications for national integration." *Mediterranean Journal of Educational Studies* 5(2): 57–82.

Assal, A. and Farrell, E. (1992). "Attempts to make meaning from terror: Family, play, and school in time of civil war." *Anthropology and Education Quarterly* 23(4): 275–90.

Bush, K. and Saltarelli, D. (eds) (2000). *The Two Faces of Education in Ethnic Conflict: Towards a Peacebuilding Education for Children*. Florence: UNICEF Innocenti Insight.

Deeb, L. (2006). *An Enchanted Modern: Gender and Public Piety in Shi`i Lebanon*. Princeton, NJ: Princeton University Press.

Euro-Trends (2009). *Study on Governance Challenges for Education in Fragile Situations: Lebanon Country Report*. Brussels: European Commission.

Fortna, B. (2002). *Imperial Classroom: Islam, the State, and Education in the Late Ottoman Empire*. Oxford: Oxford University Press.

Galtung, J. (1969). "Violence, peace, and peace research." *Journal of Peace Research* 6(3): 167–91.

Global Coalition to Protect Education from Attack [GCPEA] (n.d.), "Goals and recommendations." Available at: http://www.protectingeducation.org/.

Kelly, T. and White, C. (2006). *The UN Response to the Lebanon Crisis: An OCHA Lesson Learning Paper*. New York: UN Office for Coordination of Humanitarian Affairs. Available at: http://ochanet.unocha.org/p/Documents/Lebanon_Lesson_Learning_Review_final.pdf.

Khalaf, S. (2002). *Civil and Uncivil Violence in Lebanon: A History of the Internationalization of Communal Conflict*. New York: Columbia University Press.

Larkin, C. (2010). "Beyond the war? The Lebanese postmemory experience." *International Journal of Middle East Studies* 42(4): 615–35.

Makdisi, U. (2000). *The Culture of Sectarianism: Community, History and Violence in Nineteenth-Century Ottoman Lebanon*. Berkeley: University of California Press.

Mundy, K. and Dryden-Peterson, S. (eds) (2011). *Educating Children in Conflict Zones: Research, Policy, and Practice for Systemic Change—A Tribute to Jackie Kirk*. New York and London: Teachers College Press.

Novelli, M. and Smith, A. (2011). *The Role of Education in Peacebuilding: A Synthesis Report of Findings from Lebanon, Nepal, and Sierra Leone*. New York: UNICEF.

O'Malley, B. (2010). *Education Under Attack*. Paris: UNESCO.

Pybus, L. and Jacoby, T. (2011). "Youth in situations of violence and armed conflict," in *A Generation on the Move: Insights into the Conditions,Aspirations and Activism of Arab Youth* (Executive Summary). Beirut: Issam Fares Institute, American University of Beirut, pp. 40–4.

Salti, N. and Chaaban, J. (2010). "The role of sectarianism in the allocation of public expenditure in postwar Lebanon." *International Journal of Middle East Studies* 42(4): 637–55.

Smith, A. and Vaux, T. (2003). *Education, Conflict and International Development*. London: UK Department for International Development.

Tueni, G. (1990). "Reflections from the Republic of Tombs" [in Arabic]. *An-Nahar*. Beirut: An-Nahar.

UN (2010). *Monitoring and Reporting Mechanism on Grave Violations Against Children in Situations of Armed Conflict*. Available at: http://www.unrol.org/files/39.%20MRM%20Field%20Manual%2016-04-10-1.pdf.

UNDP (1997). *A Profile of Sustainable Human Development in Lebanon: The Displaced and Development*. Available at: http://www.undp.org.lb/programme/governance/advocacy/nhdr/nhdr97/.

—(2007). *Poverty, Growth, and Income Distribution in Lebanon*. Beirut: UNDP.

UNESCO (2010). *Protecting Education from Attack*. Paris: UNESCO.

—(2011). Education for All Global Monitoring Report 2011. *The Hidden Crisis: Armed Conflict and Education*. Paris: UNESCO.

Zakharia, Z. (2004). "How schools cope with war: A case study of Lebanon," in D. Burde, T. Arnstein, C. Pagen, and Z. Zakharia (eds), *Education in Emergencies and Post-Conflict Situations: Problems, Responses, and Possibilities*. New York: Society for International Education, pp. 107–17.

—(2011). *The Role of Education in Peacebuilding: Case Study—Lebanon*. New York: UNICEF.

Change 4 Me? Young Refugees' and Migrants' Research on Social Inclusion in London

3

Aoife O'Higgins and Rosalind Evans

Chapter Outline

The United Nations High Commissioner for Refugees estimates that there are some 33 million people of concern around the world and that half are children (United Nations High Commissioner for Refugees, 2012). A relatively small but significant proportion of these children and young people arrive in the United Kingdom every year (Home Office, 2012); many are forced migrants and refugees who arrive with their families or to reunite with family members while some also migrate unaccompanied by parents or carers. This chapter looks at the circumstances of children and young people migrating to the United Kingdom, including refugees, asylum seekers, migrants, Roma and trafficked children, and focuses on their experiences of education. First, we look at who young refugees and migrants are and their circumstances in the United Kingdom. In a review of the literature, we examine refugee and migrant children's experiences of formal education in schools and further education colleges. These include barriers to access and support, the significance of education and finally, the politics of education. This review serves as a context to introduce several small research projects, some of which the authors were involved with at the Children's Society: Count Us In (Franks, 2006) and Change 4 Me (2010). We also present findings from an initial evaluation of the Feel Free project, a peer-led capacity building project. The three projects used participatory research methods to explore the educational experiences of refugee and migrant children accessing The Children's Society projects and to consider how these needs can be met. The research finds that young people value educational opportunities provided to them though they face a number of barriers to success and integration in line with the literature. Across projects, young people expressed the wish that they be treated in the same way other young people are and not be singled out by their immigration status.

Who are migrant children and young people in the United Kingdom?

Migrant children and young people are not a homogenous group; they come from many countries around the world, belong to hundreds of ethnicities, speak thousands of languages and belong to various religious groups. Their experiences are also vastly diverse, including their experiences of migration and integration. As they arrive in the United Kingdom, factors such as their reasons for traveling to the United Kingdom and their route of travel or entry determines their immigration status. They may be refugees and asylum seekers, new migrants, undocumented children, illegal entrants, Roma or trafficked children, for example. Some young people may also be trafficked into the United Kingdom and claim asylum. Young people may be accompanied by parents, carers, siblings or other family members or be unaccompanied. Their immigration status and family situation may change over time; for example, they may be granted refugee status and eventually become British citizens or be refused asylum and become undocumented. Children may also become separated from their parents or caregivers in the United Kingdom (if there is a family breakdown). Immigration and asylum legislation is complex and migrant and refugee children face a number of important barriers to successful settlement in the United Kingdom; an overview of these issues is discussed below to provide some context for their educational experiences.

Refugee children

To be recognized as refugees by the state, and therefore be granted leave to remain in the United Kingdom, young people or their guardians must submit an application for asylum to the United Kingdom Border Agency (UKBA). Their claim should meet the requirements of the 1951 Geneva Convention, which states that a refugee is someone who:

> owing to well-founded fear of being persecuted for reasons of race, religion, nationality, membership of a particular social group or political opinion, is outside the country of his nationality and is unable or, owing to such fear, is unwilling to avail himself of the protection of that country; or who, not having a nationality and being outside the country of his former habitual residence as a result of such events, is unable or, owing to such fear, is unwilling to return to it (United Nations High Commissioner for Refugees, 2012).

Accompanied asylum-seeking children

Young people who arrive with their parents are classified as dependents on their parents' application. UKBA provides the family with minimal financial support and accommodation outside of London on a no-choice basis (UKBA, 2012a). While the family's application for asylum remains under consideration by UKBA, children are entitled to free education until the age of 18, but young people are not allowed to work or claim any public funds (e.g., education bursaries) (UKBA, 2012a). Accompanied asylum-seeking children and young people have limited access to healthcare and other public services (e.g., specialist mental health services) (Dorling, 2012). Their right to remain in the United Kingdom is determined by their guardian's application, so accompanied asylum-seeking children will only be granted asylum if their carer makes a successful application. If or when the family is granted refugee status, they are broadly entitled to the same employment, education and welfare rights as British citizens of their age (Dorling, 2012). When an application is refused, UKBA normally seeks to return the family to their country of origin.

Unaccompanied asylum-seeking children

Applicants under the age of 18 can claim asylum in their own right (unaccompanied by someone who has parental responsibility); they are then categorized as unaccompanied asylum-seeking children (UASC) or unaccompanied minors, as per government policy (UKBA, 2012b). In the last decade, some 10,000 children have made applications for asylum in the United Kingdom without a parent or guardian (Home Office, 2012). Statistics show that the majority of applications for asylum from unaccompanied minors are refused every year (Home Office, 2012); however, where there are no adequate reception arrangements in their country of origin, they are granted discretionary leave to remain (DLR) until they are 17.5 years old (UKBA, 2012b).

Unaccompanied minors are referred to the local authority children's services for accommodation and welfare support (Dorling, 2012). Official statistics show that one in three unaccompanied minors have their age disputed by UKBA or children's services (Home Office, 2012). In these cases, an in-depth assessment is carried out to determine the approximate age of the young person. Like many areas of social work that involve migrant children, age assessments are a complex process (Crawley, 2007; Hjern et al., 2012). If it is accepted that young people are under the age of 18, children's services have a legal duty to provide them accommodation and welfare support under the provisions of section 20 of the Children Act 1989 (Dorling, 2012), unless a young person specifically refuses such support (they should then be provided a lower level of support under section 17 of the same act). Unaccompanied minors under the age of 16 are usually placed in a foster home (Wade et al., 2005), while those over 16 may be placed in foster care or semi-independent accommodation (shared flats, for example). Social workers, foster carers and other support workers should provide support to access to other services such as health and education. Whether they are granted refugee status or discretionary leave to remain, unaccompanied minors are entitled to broadly the same services as citizen children (Dorling, 2012).

Other asylum-seeking and refugee children

An important number of children also migrate in the United Kingdom on a family reunion visa; that is, where their parents or guardians are granted leave to remain and apply for their dependents to join them. In 2010, there were more children arriving through this channel than children claiming asylum on arrival in the United Kingdom (Home Office, 2011); yet, these children are absent from literature or policy. While their status confers them a number of rights (to work and access services), many children find themselves in great difficulty in the case of family breakdown. They may approach or be referred to social services, but may face a number of barriers to accessing such support (O'Higgins, 2012).

A number of children are also trafficked into the United Kingdom every year (Dorling, 2012). They may claim asylum or submit an application for leave to remain on human rights grounds. Trafficked children are usually referred to social services for support, but few specialist services exist to provide them with the tailored support they may need (Dorling, 2012).

Evidence shows that refugee children are at significant risk of developing mental health problems because of the adversity they face (Bronstein and Montgomery, 2011; Fazel et al., 2012; Huemer et al., 2009). Parents and carers can act as a protective mechanism; therefore, children who are unaccompanied face greater risks (Bean et al., 2007; Fazel et al., 2012). Mental health problems, combined with a number of barriers to accessing services, may render these children and young people vulnerable. This is generally how they are characterized in literature (Crawley, 2010; Harrell-Bond, 1999; Maegusuku-Hewett et al., 2007). However, research also demonstrates that a significant number of refugee children do not suffer from mental health problems (Bronstein and Montgomery, 2011). It is also important to consider the different ways in which young people may be vulnerable as well as resilient, which may occur in different situations or in relation to different people (Clark, 2007). This tension between vulnerability and resilience is important because it points to the diverse needs of these young people and the different approaches to supporting them. By neglecting to explore the reasons why some refugee and asylum-seeking children do not suffer from mental health problems, we may fail to develop programmes that adequately respond to the needs of all refugee young people (Clark, 2007; Maegusuku-Hewett et al., 2007; O'Higgins, 2012).

Migrant children

There are many migrant children who do not claim asylum. Roma children, for example, no longer need to claim asylum where they are from countries that acceded to the European Union. European migrants are entitled to work in the United Kingdom, but access to benefits varies for different countries (Cullen et al., 2008).

Children also come to the United Kingdom from countries outside the European Union as dependents on their parents' visas. A number of children also enter illegally with or without parents or carers. Unless they claim asylum, the state does not provide welfare support to migrants who are not European. They have no recourse to public funds and are dependent on the income of their parents. If they become destitute, they may depend on the charity of community organizations, churches and social networks (Pinter, 2012; Sigona and Hughes, 2010).

Migrant children may also become the responsibility of local authority children's services where there is a family breakdown, though family reunification may be sought.

There is a dearth of literature on the needs, experiences and circumstances of migrant young people who have not, or whose parents have not, claimed asylum (Sigona and Hughes, 2010). It is unclear how many such children are in the United Kingdom, and in particular, how many are overstayers or undocumented (Sigona and Hughes, 2010; 2012). *No Way Out, No Way In*, a recent report on undocumented migrant children and families, sheds some light on the difficulties many encounter while accessing education, health services and other public services (Sigona and Hughes, 2012).

Describing and characterizing migrant children according to their immigration status is problematic because it creates fixed categories that do not reflect the experiences of many of these young people. For example, a child may claim asylum with his family, but move out when the family unit breaks down. The young person's immigration status may continue to be dependent on their family's or a separate application could be submitted. Conversely, if an unaccompanied minor is granted refugee status and finds an older sibling in the United Kingdom, the term 'unaccompanied asylum-seeking child' may not be appropriate to describe their circumstances. Categories that describe children according to their immigration status or their family situation on entry to the United Kingdom fail to reflect the changing and evolving situations of migrant children. Therefore, the approach that attempts to understand the experiences of children and young people beyond what is conferred by their immigration status was core to the research carried out for this chapter.

The education of migrant and refugee children in the United Kingdom

Entitlements

Irrespective of immigration status, children and young people under the age of 16 should be enrolled at a local educational institution in the same way citizen children are.

Unaccompanied minors who are in the care of children's services should be placed as a priority in a suitable school (Brownlees and Finch, 2010; Dorling, 2012). Young people who are supported by a local authority should be placed as a priority and according to their abilities in a suitable local school (Dorling, 2012). Those who are over 16 are enrolled in further education colleges. Children living with their parents apply to schools in the same way British children do, via the local authority (Dorling, 2012).

Many migrant young people do not speak English when they arrive in the United Kingdom and may then be placed in English for Speakers of Other Languages (ESOL) classes in further education colleges; depending on their age and the resources available, younger children may be offered targeted support in their local school. Other rights and entitlements (free school meals, uniforms, travel expenses, etc.) vary as the immigration status changes (Dorling, 2012). Migrants whose parents have no recourse to public funds, however, will not be entitled to free school meals or uniforms.

Accessing education

Refugee and migrant children may experience a number of obstacles to accessing education. Many arrive in the United Kingdom in the middle of the school year and are unable to enrol because their local schools are full (Arnot and Pinson, 2005; Brownlees and Finch, 2010; Dorling, 2012). Migrant parents may be unfamiliar with enrolment procedures and find these complex. Families may also be required to provide documents that they do not have (Sigona and Hughes, 2012). In addition, many parents have limited language skills, which makes it difficult for them to adequately complete application forms and communicate with officials (Sigona and Hughes, 2012).

The access of refugee children to schooling may be hampered by similar difficulties. Those who are unaccompanied must rely on social workers to apply to schools or colleges on their behalf (Brownlees and Finch, 2010; Dorling, 2012). Because many young people have their age disputed and the assessment process is often protracted, young people may spend some time in the United Kingdom unable to attend a school or college. This may be because they have no identification to prove their identity and have no responsible adult to support them (Arnot and Pinson, 2005; Brownlees and Finch, 2010; Sigona and Hughes, 2012). Some children and young people are therefore left to approach schools and colleges and advocate for themselves; however, access may still be restricted for those without documents (O'Higgins, 2012).

Asylum-seeking children who live with their parents in UKBA accommodation are often moved and at short notice; as a result, children may need to change schools. This creates difficulties for enrolment and for children adapting to new environments.

Barriers to success

Many young migrants face significant difficulties in adapting and adjusting to their new educational environment, once they are enrolled. Young people with limited language or writing skills may struggle to adapt to the demands of the British education system. Migrants from rural communities in countries such as Afghanistan, for example, may have had little experience of formal education or an interrupted education due to war or abrupt departure from their homes. However, some research evidence shows that success may not be linked to prior educational experiences, but rather to the support available and quality of education in the United Kingdom (Brownlees and Finch, 2010).

Many young migrants, and particularly young refugees, may also have high absenteeism due to appointments with solicitors, UKBA or their social workers (Arnot and Pinson, 2005; Brownlees and Finch, 2010; Dorling, 2012). While schools and teachers may be understanding and flexible, absences may impact on continuity and educational success. Other practical difficulties include precarious or overcrowded housing, lack of funds for basic necessities such as food as well as travel expenses to school. These difficulties are often compounded in rural areas that have few support services to enable migrant children to overcome these difficulties.

Undocumented and irregular migrant parents enrolling their children may worry that their details will be communicated to UKBA for removal and it is likely that such anxieties will be shared by the children and young people too (Humphries, 2004; Sigona and Hughes, 2012). Accompanied and unaccompanied asylum-seeking children may also be anxious if their immigration status is undetermined. Indeed, if they are in the United Kingdom with their parents, a refused application could lead to destitution or removal from the United Kingdom. Unaccompanied asylum-seeking children are usually given the right to remain until they reach the age of 17.5, but they may still be going through appeals or worrying about what will happen when their leave to remain expires (Barrie and Mendes, 2011; Stanley, 2001).

Emotional difficulties may also affect the children's ability to concentrate in school. Various studies show that refugee children are likely to experience some psychological difficulties in the United Kingdom related to their past experiences (Bronstein and Montgomery, 2011; Fazel et al., 2012; Huemer et al., 2009). This may include experiences of war, persecution, harassment, torture, rape or witnessing violence towards family members or their community. Children who are affected by posttraumatic stress disorder experience disrupted sleep, flashbacks and intrusive memories and it is likely that this will affect their education (Fazel et al., 2012). While it is not the majority of refugee children who have mental health problems, studies show that most young refugees are affected by anxieties about the past, their families and their well-being and uncertain future (Fazel et al., 2012; Sigona and Hughes, 2012).

Finally, racism and discrimination as well as bullying are rife in many schools in the United Kingdom (Arnot and Pinson, 2005; Sigona and Hughes, 2012; Stanley, 2001). This includes exclusion, isolation, name-calling, intimidation, harassment, being singled out, threats of and actual violence. Refugee and migrant children may suffer from bullying because of their ethnicity or (imputed) immigration status. Given the current prevailing negative discourse about migrants in the United Kingdom, which we discuss further below, it is no surprise that this extends to the playground. Such experiences may further curtail migrant children's abilities to successfully integrate.

There exist a number of organizations and individuals from public and voluntary sector agencies who work with refugee and migrant children. These include social workers, support workers, specialist tutors or other education professionals, charities (e.g., the Refugee Council Children's Panel) and community groups. However, government austerity measures have resulted in service closures, and services that remain open are under increasing pressure. This has led to concerns that refugee and migrant children will find it increasingly difficult to access services and support, including education that can increase their chances of success (Hill, 2011; Migrants' Rights Network, 2012).

It is likely that these various issues are intertwined in the lives of young people and that different risk and protective factors affect refugee and migrant children's educational success in different ways. For example, there is evidence that families and supportive adults act as a protective factor for forced migrant children (Fazel et al., 2012). This means that children living with their parents may fare better than those who are unaccompanied, and those who are unaccompanied and living with a supportive foster carer may have greater chances of success than unaccompanied young people living in bed and breakfast or hostel accommodation on their own (Brownlees and Finch, 2010; Chase et al., 2008; Wade et al., 2005).

The significance of education for migrant children

Research suggests education can play a crucial role in mediating young migrants' well-being and accelerating their integration in the United Kingdom (Arnot and Pinson, 2005; Chase et al., 2008; Dorling, 2012; Wade et al., 2005); education can help migrant young people find a place in their new community, make friends, develop networks and may also serve as a coping mechanism for those suffering from mental health problems or anxiety (Fazel et al., 2012).

A review of the research in this area highlights the central role of education in the lives of young migrants in the United Kingdom (Fazel et al., 2012; Hek, 2005). Education can promote social inclusion and enable young migrants to make friends and develop social networks (Arnot and Pinson, 2005; Brownlees and Finch, 2010; Chase et al., 2008; Wade et al., 2005); the school or college environment as well as learning processes also contribute to the emotional and developmental needs of children and young people as well as to their overall well-being. Indeed, education can support the integration of children, and as their skills and knowledge develop, they gain more control over their lives (e.g., newly acquired language skills allow them greater independence from interpreters and professionals), which in turn, increases confidence and self-esteem and promotes well-being (Chase et al., 2008). A longitudinal study also found that children who were in education at the point of follow-up (nine years from baseline) had a lower prevalence of mental health issues than those who were not in education (Montgomery, 2010). However, there is insufficient evidence as of yet to draw definitive conclusions on the link between educational success and mental health (Fazel et al., 2012). Attending school or college is also widely reported as an effective coping mechanism for refugee children (Brownlees and Finch, 2010; Fazel et al., 2012). Many children and their parents view school and college as a safe environment, and teachers are reported to be sensitive, supportive and helpful with their difficulties (Sigona and Hughes, 2012). Research also highlights the value of routine, structure and professional support for children in schools (Hek, 2005). Young people explain that they enjoy school because its routine distracts them from the anxieties they have about the past, present difficulties or uncertain future (Arnot and Pinson, 2005; Chase et al., 2008; Hek, 2005; Wade et al., 2005). Finally, education often plays this central role because it is seen as a gateway to success for the future, away from the troubles of the past (Arnot and Pinson, 2005; Sigona and Hughes, 2012). Education is therefore a key post-migration investment for children and young people and their families.

The politics of education for refugee and migrant young people

Many schools and local education authorities have strategic policies on the inclusion of migrant and refugee children. However, the implementation of anti-discriminatory policies varies from school to school (Arnot and Pinson, 2005). Variations may exist because of resources in place, the perceived need for (or lack of) such policies and the will of individual schools and head teachers.

The marginalization of migrant young people in schools reflects some of the broader realities for migrants in British society (Boyden, 2009). Increasingly restrictive and punitive measures towards migrants are reflected in policies that affect migrant and refugee children. Indeed, there continue to be concerns that refugee children are treated primarily as migrants, rather than as children (Crawley, 2006); successive governments appear reluctant to extend the measures that safeguard citizen children to those who are asylum seekers and migrants. For instance, the safeguarding provisions of the Children Act 2004 and UN Convention on the Rights of the Child were initially limited to citizen children though this has since been overturned (Dorling, 2012). Forced migrants, including children, are perceived to be a burden on public services such as health services and schools. Providing resources to services specifically to support these young people may, therefore, also be resisted. Boyden (2009) argues that education objectives and policies in the United Kingdom aim to foster a nationalist ideology and promote social cohesion and loyalty to the state, first and foremost. However, it is not clear what the role of refugees and migrants is in this narrative, as the public discourse on migrants tends to exclude them from mainstream British society. In their research on refugees in education, Arnot and Pinson (2005) highlight the efforts of schools and individual teachers seeking to develop a sense of compassion and morality in their pupils, thus challenging the government rhetoric. Through these approaches to education, Boyden (2009) concludes that schools may be the best place to 'broker the effective integration of young forced migrants within British society today' (p. 271); education can promote social justice and tolerance, thus facilitating the integration and reducing the marginalization of migrant children. Therefore, despite the continuing challenges faced by these young people in accessing and succeeding in education, schools provide an ideal locus for further study of their experiences and facilitating their integration.

Refugee and migrant young people's experiences of education

The Children's Society initiated three pieces of research and advocacy about migrant young people's experiences of education in the United Kingdom. Count Us In was initiated by the research unit and Change 4 Me was developed at New Londoners, a London-based Children's Society project. The Feel Free project was initiated by staff and young people of the New Londoners project. These used participatory research methods to equip young migrants with the skills and confidence to explore their experiences of school and college and investigate those of their peers. In this section, we describe the research projects, the research methods and the approaches used, and present the findings.

Count Us In! Change 4 Me? Feel Free! Three participatory education projects for refugee and migrant young people

Count Us In was initiated by The Children's Society in 2006. The project surveyed 106 migrant children and young people about their experiences of access to and achievement in education in the United Kingdom (Franks, 2006). It included interviews with 11 professionals. The project also trained seven migrant young people in research skills, and they conducted interviews with 40 children about their experiences of education.

The second project, Change 4 Me, was undertaken to evaluate a national initiative – Leading Edge – that was launched following the Count Us In research at The Children's Society. Change 4 Me gathered further qualitative information about the issues affecting refugees' and asylum seekers' experiences of secondary education. The Leading Edge initiative aimed to improve access to and achievement in secondary schools for young refugees and asylum seekers in six locations across England. In collaboration with education providers and local authority education professionals, the delivery of after school clubs, peer mentoring and social activities were organized to strengthen the social and support networks of newly arrived young people.

In 2009–2010, the Leading Edge work in London was led by Rosalind Evans at The Children's Society; she also initiated the Change 4 Me research in collaboration with young people attending the project. The Change 4 Me research project fed into the national evaluation of the Leading Edge Initiative and contributed to The Children's Society's efforts to influence educational policy and practice.

The third project we discuss is the Feel Free Project. The findings presented here are extracted from an initial evaluation of Feel Free. The Feel Free initiative was developed in collaboration with young people; it drew on learning from previous research, including Count Us In and Change 4 Me. The Feel Free Project was established after a small group of refugee and migrant young people successfully applied for a grant to create a project led by young people. The successful bid initially proposed that a group of young refugees – named Feel Free – would develop and deliver workshops to teach their peers better independent living skills (cooking, cleaning, budgeting, looking for work, etc.). Local authority children's services are mandated to prepare young people in their care for living independently, but such support and training is not delivered consistently and many Feel Free members reported being ill equipped to live alone. Young people who are not looked after by social services should receive support to live independently from their parents and families; however, the Feel Free group felt that these young people would also benefit from third-party workshops. After some weeks of planning and preparation, Feel Free decided that their group sessions should not be restricted to refugee young people, but tailored to cater to all young persons needing support to develop independent living skills. Other steps were taken to make their work more inclusive, such as recruiting citizen young people to become part of the steering committee. This strategic move by the members of the Feel Free group was not welcomed by some organizations that limit access of their activities to young refugees and specifically only those who are categorized as unaccompanied minors under the age of 18. However, the Feel Free group felt strongly that the needs of young refugees did not widely differ from those of citizen young people with regard to independent living skills. They also stated that they did not want to be categorized in isolation in this way.

Research methods

Count Us In and Change 4 Me were both specifically designed as research projects, whereas the findings from Feel Free, which we present here, are extracted from an evaluation of the work of young people, conducted by staff from The Children's Society.

All initiatives used participatory research tools and methods. This is based on the recognition of the agency and the abilities of migrant young people to participate in processes that affect their lives. The research also aims to be an integral part of the empowerment process for them. Participatory research methods in studies with children have become increasingly popular over the last 20 years. This has resulted, in part, from transformations in the way children are perceived by social scientists. The new paradigm of childhood studies encouraged greater recognition of young people's social agency and capacities (James and Prout, 1997). Additionally, the United Nations Convention on the Rights of the Child accords children the rights to information, assembly and to participation in decision-making processes that affect them, and its widespread influence has inspired new opportunities for young people to be consulted directly and even to conduct their own research projects with support from adults.

In Count Us In and Change for Me, young people were recruited and trained as peer researchers. Here, we focus on Change 4 Me as the participatory process was developed and facilitated entirely by one of the authors (see Franks, 2006, for the research methods and demographic details of participants of the Count Us In project).

In December 2009, 18 young people from four different schools spent a weekend learning how to conduct interviews and run group research activities using drama and art. They chose a name for this group – Change 4 Me – and decided what they hoped to achieve through participating in this project. They aimed to learn new skills, to share different views and ideas with others and to do something for refugees at that time and in the future. The researchers chose to explore a different topic in each school. These topics included finding out what makes new students feel welcome at school, how young refugees feel about education, how bullying affects refugee students, and whether or not young refugees' hopes and expectations of education in the United Kingdom were met. The young researchers decided what questions to ask other students and teachers and conducted interviews during lunchtimes and after school. In January 2010, they participated in a residential weekend workshop with other young refugees, who became participants in research activities, such as group discussions and drama. Following data collection and analysis, the young people contributed to writing a report.

The data from the Feel Free evaluation was gathered through individual interviews and a focus group discussion following a workshop delivered by the Feel Free group to other young people.

What the research found

Access to education

Count Us In and Change 4 Me reported some challenges faced by migrant and refugee young people with respect to accessing education. Young people and teachers reported that many young people had had to wait for a school place after they arrived, and in some cases for a long time, when they arrived in the middle of the school year. In the Count Us In project, 15 to 17-year-olds had experienced longer waits; this includes a significant number of young people in the care of social services. In some areas, practitioners reported long waiting lists and in one local authority, there were over 100 refugee children waiting for a school place (Franks, 2006). Practitioners supporting young people believed the reason for this was limited college resources. Some colleges were also reluctant to enrol young people into year 11 because of the impact on GCSEs. It may also be the case that new arrivals do not have the level of English required to join those preparing for GCSEs. However, given that many of the young people who arrive without a parent or carer are 16 years old, the reluctance of colleges to admit young people into year 11 significantly impacts this group of young people.

There is also a suggestion from the Count Us In research that different ethnic groups face different problems, for example, Roma in Newham (London) were found to be particularly marginalized.

Importance of education and barriers to success

Young people in all projects shared their enthusiasm for education and school and the ambition to do well and get good jobs; however, they faced a number of barriers to success. Many aimed for high attendance, but had records of absenteeism. The reasons for this included – young people living alone with no one to help them develop a routine, such as waking up in the morning; having important appointments to attend during school hours; poor housing and limited space to study or do homework; having care responsibilities; and language and cultural barriers.

Language and cultural barriers meant young people could not engage well with education, got bored and were limited in their ability to build social networks. It also increased the likelihood that they would be bullied. Young people described the process of acculturation and the need to bridge the cultural gap as necessary in order to successfully integrate into a new school and system.

Several young people also mentioned the lack of support during the integration and acculturation process. Parents did not always understand the United Kingdom's school system and those who were unaccompanied received little support from social workers. Young people from the Feel Free group also talked about limited social services and parental support to develop independent living skills. Young people who recently arrived in the United Kingdom may therefore have little support outside of school in terms of adapting to their new learning environments.

All projects reported significant problems with bullying. Most young people had either experienced bullying themselves or witnessed incidences, such as saying 'I got bullied many times in school' (Hazzazzi, Interview, 2010). In one case, young people reported suicidal intentions. Young people in Count Us In and Change 4 Me provided examples of bullying, including name-calling, teasing, harassment, etc.; this was perceived to be on account of the young people's accents, religion and religious practices (wearing a head scarf, for example). However, it was not always clear if young people were bullied because they were not British or specifically because of their immigration status.

While teachers mostly recognized this as a problem, young people reported more bullying than teachers and suggested that some teachers did not know or understand bullying of migrant young people or that they ignored it. The Change 4 Me project, which included interviews with teachers, highlighted their understanding of the impact of bullying and their efforts to challenge it. Pupils and teachers reported that bullying increased the isolation and marginalization of migrant and refugee young people as well as impacted their self-esteem and mental health.

Young people make suggestions about improving the integration of new arrivals

Young people had a number of ideas to improve access to newly arrived migrants and refugees in schools. Most young people found teachers supportive and understanding of their difficulties (e.g., about their having to attend appointments during school hours) and young people's concerns about bullying. However, it was stated by several young people that teachers should make more effort to stop bullying and that schools should develop strategies to reduce instances of bullying, for example, by increasing cultural awareness through school displays, social activities and classroom-based activities. Participants proposed that students who bully others should also be provided support.

Young people suggested that parents should be engaged and involved more, as their relationships with the school might foster a more supportive environment. Participants also felt that families and migrant and refugee children should receive more support, for example that all pupils should get free school meals. Young people also suggested that teachers should be able to signpost those who needed further support outside of school.

Finally, young people from the three projects explicitly stated that they did not want to be singled out because of their immigration status, as the Feel Free group already demonstrated this in the course of the project development itself. The Feel Free group reflected on their experiences and concluded that independent living skills training was important for young people, regardless of their nationality or immigration status. Young people in the Count Us In and Change 4 Me projects agreed; most young people felt that they needed tailored support to facilitate their integration, which might include extra classroom assistance or language support, but they did not want to be taught separately or singled out. Many feared that being singled out would result in bullying or further marginalization. Participants also believed that their needs were not so different to their peers.

Conclusion

Listening to the accounts of young migrants can enhance practitioners' understanding of their experiences and thus improve services, including the delivery of education (Kelly, 2012).

The experiences of young people who took part in the projects discussed in this chapter echoed those in literature on young migrants and their education in the United Kingdom. The findings highlight young people's difficulties in accessing education and the barriers to success. Young people are aware and cognizant of other challenges they face, including bullying and marginalization. However, they are able to suggest strategies that they, teachers or schools could adopt to overcome these. These findings thus shed light on the complex experiences of young migrants in London and the tension between their vulnerability and their resilience to adversity.

The strategies proposed by young people may provide a key to supporting their education and improving their integration (hypotheses should be generated for further research). Findings – common to the three projects – demonstrate that many migrant and refugee young people are reluctant to identify themselves, or for others to identify them, according to their immigration status. Research on refugee children echoes this finding and advocates that terminology on migrant children should change to reflect this (Bokhari, 2012); for example the term 'separated children' is proposed to describe forced migrant children who are in the United Kingdom without their main carer.

This finding suggests that service providers, including schools and colleges, should consider supporting young migrants in ways that do not single them out by immigration status. This may reduce bullying and other forms of stigmatization. It may also contribute to promoting young migrants' well-being and integration in schools. Many support organizations outside of schools are targeted services and cater to the needs of specific migrant populations. Evidence about whether targeted or universal services are more effective remains equivocal. To our knowledge, there is no evidence on whether targeted services engender further discrimination in communities or not. However, the findings here suggest that there is an important group of migrant young people who experience targeted services as disempowering. If important numbers of young migrants are reluctant to be identified by their immigration status, it is likely that they will reluctantly, if at all, access services for refugees or migrants only. These findings do not seek to discourage schools from offering specialist support to refugee and migrant children; indeed many young migrants find the experience of starting school difficult and need further support, as shown above.

It is not within the remit of this chapter to determine a best practice approach for schools, but to highlight the perspectives of young migrants on education. Yet, the findings in the chapter may suggest that it is appropriate to provide universal support services within which specialist and targeted support are offered to migrant young people. For example, many local authority children's services teams now are universal, but include several specialist refugee workers. This may allow for migrant young people to be integrated with other young people, while receiving specialist support to facilitate the process of integration and empower them. While this approach does not directly address issues of bullying, racism or marginalization, it allows migrant young people to exercise control over their migration narrative and develop an identity that is not based on their immigration status. This may then lead to lower levels of discrimination and bullying and promote the integration of this group of children and young people. Schools and colleges may be particularly well placed to adopt such an approach, because, unlike most other services migrant young people access regularly, admission is not decided on the basis of immigration status.

Questions for reflection

- Why do you think education is so important to young migrants?
- Do you think refugee children are vulnerable, resilient or both? Can you explain why and how you think this might affect their education?
- Can you explain the concept of 'discourse' and identify what the popular refugee discourse is? Can you think of reasons why this discourse exists and how it may be relevant to young migrants in education?

Further reading

Sigona, N. and Hughes, V. (2010). Being children and undocumented in the UK: A background paper. *Society*. Oxford.

An interesting paper which explores some of the experiences of refugee children in the United Kingdom and politics of administrative labels.

Arnot, M. and Pinson, H. (2005). *The Education of Asylum-Seeker & Refugee Children*. Cambridge, UK. Retrieved from http://www.educ.cam.ac.uk/people/staff/arnot/AsylumReportFinal.pdf.

This is a good overview of the issues young refugees face in the United Kingdom and with special regard to their education.

Boyden, J. (2009). What place the politics of compassion in education surrounding non-citizen children? *Educational Review 61*(3): 265–76.

A thought provoking article on the role of education for migrants in British society.

Wade, J., Mitchell, F. and Baylis, G. (2005). *Unaccompanied Asylum Seeking Children: The Response of Social Work Services*. London: British Association of Adoption and Fostering (BAAF).

An important book on the experiences and rights and entitlements of young refugees in the United Kingdom.

References

Arnot, M. and Pinson, H. (2005). *The Education of Asylum-Seeker & Refugee Children.* Cambridge, UK. Retrieved from http://www.educ.cam.ac.uk/people/staff/arnot/AsylumReportFinal.pdf.

Barrie, L. and Mendes, P. (2011). The experiences of unaccompanied asylum-seeking children in and leaving the out-of-home care system in the UK and Australia: A critical review of the literature. *International Social Work* 54(4): 485–503. doi:10.1177/0020872810389318.

Bean, T., Derluyn, I., Eurelings-Bontekoe, E., Broekaert, E. and Spinhoven, P. (2007). Comparing psychological distress, traumatic stress reactions, and experiences of unaccompanied refugee minors with experiences of adolescents accompanied by parents. *The Journal of nervous and mental disease* 195(4): 288–97. Retrieved from http://www.ncbi.nlm.nih.gov/pubmed/17435478.

Bokhari, F. (2012). Separated Children in the UK: Policy and Legislation. In E. Kelly and F. Bokhari (eds), *Safeguarding Children from Abroad: Refugee, Asylum Seeking and Trafficked Children in the UK.* London: Jessica Kingsley.

Boyden, J. (2009). What place the politics of compassion in education surrounding non-citizen children? *Educational Review* 61(3): 265–76. doi:10.1080/00131910903045914.

Bronstein, I. and Montgomery, P. (2011). Psychological distress in refugee children: a systematic review. *Clinical child and family psychology review* 14(1): 44–56. doi:10.1007/s10567-010-0081-0.

Brownlees, L. and Finch, N. (2010). *Levelling the playing field: A UNICEF UK report into provision of services to unaccompanied or separated migrant children in three local authority areas in England.* Retrieved from http://www.unicef.org.uk/Documents/Publications/levelling-playing-field.pdf.

Chase, E., Knight, A. and Statham, J. (2008). *The Emotional Wellbeing of Unaccompanied Young People Seeking Asylum in the UK.* London: British Association of Adoption and Fostering (BAAF).

Clark, C. R. (2007). Understanding Vulnerability: From Categories to Experiences of Young Congolese People in Uganda. *Children & Society* 21(4): 284–96. doi:10.1111/j.1099-0860.2007.00100.x.

Crawley, H. (2006). *Child First, Migrant Second: Ensuring that Every Child Matters.* London: Immigration Law Practitioners' Association (ILPA). Retrieved from http://www.ilpa.org.uk/data/resources/13270/ilpa_child_first.pdf.

—(2007). *When is a Child not a Child? Asylum, Age Disputes and the Process of Age Assessment.* London. Retrieved from www.ilpa.org.

—(2010). "No one gives you a chance to say what you are thinking": finding space for children's agency in the UK asylum system. Area 42(2): 162–9. doi:10.1111/j.1475-4762.2009.00917.x.

Cullen, S., Hayes, P. and Hughes, L. (2008). *Good Practice Guide: Working with Housed Gypsies and Travellers.* Retrieved from http://england.shelter.org.uk/__data/assets/pdf_file/0010/57772/Working_with_housed_Gypsies_and_Travellers.pdf.

Dorling, K. (2012). *Seeking Support A Guide to the Rights and Entitlements of Separated Children.* Retrieved from http://www.seekingsupport.co.uk/.

Fazel, M., Reed, R. V., Panter-Brick, C. and Stein, A. (2012). Mental health of displaced and refugee children resettled in high-income countries: risk and protective factors. *Lancet* 379(9812): 266–82. Elsevier Ltd. doi:10.1016/S0140-6736(11)60051-2.

Franks, M. (2006). *Count Us In: Young Refugees in Education.* Retrieved from http://www.childrenssociety.org.uk/sites/default/files/tcs/research_docs/Count us in - Young refugees in the education system.pdf.

Harrell-Bond, B. (1999). The experience of refugees as recipients of aid. In A. Ager (ed.), *Refugees: Perspectives on the Experience of Forced Migration.* London: Pinter, pp. 136–68.

Hek, R. (2005). *The Experiences and Needs of Refugee and Asylum Seeking Children in the UK: A Literature Review.* London. Retrieved from http://dera.ioe.ac.uk/5398/1/RR635.pdf

Hill, A. (2011). Refugee services to take a heavy hit due to 62% funding cuts. *The Guardian.* Retrieved from http://www.guardian.co.uk/world/2011/feb/01/refugee-services-heavy-hit-cuts.

Hjern, A., Brendler-Lindqvist, M. and Norredam, M. (2012). Age assessment of young asylum seekers. *Acta paediatrica (Oslo, Norway: 1992)* 101(1): 4–7. doi:10.1111/j.1651-2227.2011.02476.x.

Home Office (2011). Family Reunion Statistics.

—(2012). Immigration Statistics October - December 2011. Retrieved from http://www.homeoffice.gov.uk/publications/science-research-statistics/research-statistics/immigration-asylum-research/immigration-q4-2011/?view=Standard&pubID=1007858.

Huemer, J., Karnik, N. S., Voelkl-Kernstock, S., Granditsch, E., Dervic, K., Friedrich, M. H. and Steiner, H. (2009). Mental health issues in unaccompanied refugee minors. *Child and Adolescent Psychiatry and Mental health* 3(1): 13. doi:10.1186/1753-2000-3-13.

Humphries, B. (2004). An Unacceptable Role for Social Work: Implementing Immigration Policy. *British Journal of Social Work* 34(1): 93–107. doi:10.1093/bjsw/bch007.

James, A. and Prout, A. (1997). *Constructing and reconstructing childhood: contemporary issues in the sociological study of childhood* (2nd edn). London: Falmer Press.

Kelly, E. (2012). Listening to Separated Children. In E. Kelly and F. Bokhari (eds), *Safeguarding Children from Abroad: Refugee, Asylum Seeking and Trafficked Children in the UK.* London: Jessica Kingsley, pp. 135–51.

Maegusuku-Hewett, T., Dunkerley, D., Scourfield, J. and Smalley, N. (2007). Refugee Children in Wales: Coping and Adaptation in the Face of Adversity. *Children & Society* 21(4): 309–21. doi:10.1111/j.1099-0860.2007.00102.x

Migrants' Rights Network. (2012). budget cuts. Retrieved from http://www.migrantsrights.org.uk/taxonomy/term/84/0?page=2.

Montgomery, E. (2010). Trauma and resilience in young refugees: a 9-year follow-up study. *Development and Psychopathology,* 22(2), 477–89. Retrieved from http://www.ncbi.nlm.nih.gov/pubmed/20423554

O'Higgins, A. (2012). Vulnerability and agency: Beyond an irreconcilable dichotomy for social service providers working with young refugees in the UK. *New Directions for Child and Adolescent Development* 2012(136): 79–91. doi:10.1002/cad.20012.

Pinter, I. (2012). *"I don't feel human" Experiences of destitution among young refugees and migrants.* Retrieved from http://www.childrenssociety.org.uk/sites/default/files/tcs/research_docs/thechildrenssociety_idontfeelhuman_final.pdf

Sigona, N. and Hughes, V. (2010). Being children and undocumented in the UK: A background paper. *Working Paper No. 78.* Oxford: Centre on Migration Policy and Society, University of Oxford.

—(2012). *No Way Out, No Way In: Irregular migrant children and families in the UK*. Oxford. Retrieved from http://www.compas.ox.ac.uk/fileadmin/files/Publications/Reports/NO_WAY_OUT_NO_WAY_IN_FINAL.pdf

Stanley, K. (2001). *Cold Comfort - Young Separated Refugees in England.* London: Save the Children Fund.

UKBA. (2012a). Asylum Support. Retrieved a from http://www.ukba.homeoffice.gov.uk/asylum/support/.

—(2012b). Processing an asylum application from a child. Retrieved b from http://www.ukba.homeoffice.gov.uk/sitecontent/documents/policyandlaw/asylumprocessguidance/specialcases/guidance/processingasylumapplication1.pdf?view=Binary

United Nations High Commissioner for Refugees. (2012). Convention and Protocol relating to the status of refugees. Retrieved from http://www.unhcr.org/3b66c2aa10.html.

Wade, J., Mitchell, F. and Baylis, G. (2005). *Unaccompanied Asylum Seeking Children: The Response of Social Work Services*. London: British Association of Adoption and Fostering (BAAF).

Education and Disadvantaged Children in India

4

Mohammad Akhtar Siddiqui

Chapter Outline

The context of education in India

India is the second most populous country of the world, having 1.21 billion people (2011) and one of the fastest growing economies among the developing countries, with an annual growth rate of around 8 per cent. It constitutes a mosaic of diverse cultures, languages, religions and environments. In order to preserve this diversity the Constitution has guaranteed that every section of citizens having a distinct language, script or culture of its own shall have the right to conserve the same.

That the intrinsic value of education has been deeply appreciated in India is evident from the centuries-old tradition of learning in the country. The Indian people also believe that in the contemporary world, education is the single most effective means of individual and national development. Only through education can democratic principles of equality of opportunity and social justice be effectively practised, and goals of peace and prosperity be achieved. Hence, they aspire that every child have access to education. Gandhi's view reflects this national belief: 'if India was to succeed in the future then education would have to be disseminated among the masses' (Richards, 2001, p. 70). The observation made in this regard by Maulana Azad, the first Minister of Education after independence, is no less relevant:

> Every individual has right to an education that will enable him to develop his faculties and live full human life. Such education is the birth right of every citizen. A state cannot claim to have discharged its duty till it has provided for every single individual means to the acquisition of knowledge and self-betterment (Singh, 2003, p. 118).

These views received full promotion in the Directive Principles to the State Policy included in the Constitution. Under Article 45, it stipulates that the state shall endeavour to provide, within a period of 10 years from the commencement of this Constitution, for the free and compulsory education of all the children until they complete the age of 14 years.

The achievement of this constitutional goal gained pace after the announcement of a National Policy on Education in 1986, and substantial funding from the federal government to the state governments for this purpose. This, together with some external assistance, supported schemes such as Operation Blackboard (Dyer, 2000), the District Primary Education Programme (DPEP), *Sarva Shiksha Abhyan*, the Mid-day Meal and others. The global resolve for Education for All, based on the idea that elementary education is a fundamental human right adopted in the Jomtien Declaration in 1990 and reiterated in the Dakar Accord in 2000, further stimulated India's efforts towards speedy universalization of elementary education. India declared elementary education as a fundamental right of children in 2002, and after federal consultations, promulgated the Right of Children for Free and Compulsory Education (RTE) Act in 2009. The act envisages compulsory provision of education of acceptable quality to all children in the age group 6–14 years (Government of India, 2009).

Children in schools

By the school year 2009–2010, the country had opened as many as 823,162 primary schools and 367,745 upper primary/middle schools, which had enrolled 135.7 million children in classes I–V with a Gross Enrolment Ratio (GER) of 115 per cent and 59.4 million children in classes VI–VIII with a GER of 81.52 per cent. Dropout rates for 2009–2010 came down to 28.86 per cent and 42.39 per cent at primary and elementary levels from 42.60 per cent and 60.90 per cent in 1990–1991, respectively (Government of India, 2011a, p. 4). The growth rate of enrolments in elementary schools during the first decade of the twenty-first century was almost double the growth rate obtained during the last decade of the twentieth century. During the years 2006–10, the Net Enrolment Ratios (NER) in almost all states have shown a steady rise due to improved access conditions and innovative enrolment strategies. These initiatives include enrolment drives, community mobilization, maintaining a child population register in each village and child tracking on the basis of this register. The increase in NER is more prominent at the primary level. DISE data (2009–2010) indicates that only a few states such as Delhi, Jammu & Kashmir, Karnataka, Orissa, Sikkim and Uttar Pradesh have achieved high NER at the primary level, ranging between 93 per cent and 99 per cent. As against NER, the National Sample Survey (NSS) shows that the net attendance ratio (NAR) for classes I–V and VI–VIII was 84 and 59, respectively (NSSO, 2010, p. A173). NAR figures, observed the 15th Joint Review Mission (JRM), present a more accurate picture than the figures available in DISE data and the information that states collect through the village education registers because NSS collects more 'attendance' pertinent data (MHRD, 2012, p. 12); simple formal access to and enrolment in school is not sufficient to realize the potential of education through the goal of Universal Primary Education (Rizvi et al., 2007, p. 9).

However, NSS fails to capture and reflect the regularity of attendance, which is one of the important determinants of quality of learning. Despite children having been on school rolls throughout the year, they may not attend their classes regularly for a variety of reasons, such as engagement in economic activity, general lack of interest in studies, engagement with younger siblings, engagement in some family chores, ill-health, non-availability of teachers in schools, irregular functioning of schools, especially in rural areas, alienating and disrespect in relation to the sociopsychological environment in schools and other constraints. Names of such irregular and non-attending students are generally not struck off the rolls, and they are recorded as regularly attending school. In many schools in rural areas, it is observed that attendance rate in primary classes is high in the early hours of school, but dwindles significantly after the mid-day meal, as many children leave the school after eating. Partial attendance is, in effect, a form of wastage where some children drop out altogether after various periods of time.

Emphasis on quality education

Quality is a comprehensive and holistic view of education (Kumar, 2010, p. 10). Quality education means education that is relevant and contextual to the lives of the individual. Poor quality education does not help groom the children's talent and character, and does not therefore empower them to improve their capabilities and life chances. This then results in a perpetuation of their deprivation and poverty, in turn further widening the disparities in living standards within India. As technology-driven development moves forward, it makes living costlier and more complex, and if a kind of education that enables people to successfully participate in this process is not imparted, the disadvantaged children are at an even greater risk of being pushed to the margins of society in their adult life. Thus, even if access, enrolment and attendance are ensured, one will have to see whether the conditions of education offer an appropriate quality of the learning environment within which relevant learning experiences can be enjoyed.

The quality of education has, besides the suitability of the curriculum and its other correlates, also much to do with teachers who impart formal learning in schools. Their professional orientations, attitudes, values, competence and disposition towards diversities existing in their classroom can set the tone for learning. It has been rightly said that 'effective learning comes via teachers who deliver the curriculum in a way that actively engages students' understanding' (Gray, 2007, p. 106).

The National Knowledge Commission (NKC) (2007) found that in a number of states, funds were used to create 'Education Centres' (*Shiksha Kendras*) rather than proper schools. These centres employed extremely under qualified and underpaid teachers. They had around 16 per cent of the total enrolments in primary schools. The children attending were described in the official statistics as being enrolled in schools even though going to an education centre cannot be treated on a par with a proper school enrolment (NKC, 2007, p. 17). The commission also considered that the current school system is highly segmented even in government-run institutions, which need to be integrated to give all children access to school education of an acceptable quality. This is important especially from the standpoint that the government schools are the main providers of education to the deprived sections of the population, particularly children belonging to the Scheduled Castes (SC) and Scheduled Tribes (ST) (NUEPA, 2011, p. xv). Even in proper elementary schools, there were more than half a million 'contract teachers' in 2008–2009 and less than 14 per cent of them had a Bachelor of Education (B. Ed) or an equivalent degree (NUEPA, p. xvi). These teachers are paid one-fourth to one-third of the salaries of regular teachers even though they also teach full classes. As a result, they operate with a deep sense of insecurity, exploitation and dissatisfaction, which obviously impacts negatively on the quality of teaching and learning of the children. A study on para/contract teachers in Uttar Pradesh revealed that these teachers were generally unhappy with their pay and related conditions, and that they demanded better training, higher remuneration and its timely payment by authorities (Goyal, 2010, p. 325).

It is hoped that full enforcement of the RTE Act in all states will eventually resolve these issues. Some quality monitoring structure, as suggested by the Knowledge Commission (2007), also seems necessary, particularly in view of the compulsory annual promotion policy for children adopted in the RTE Act.

Out-of-school children and poverty

Despite the claim that 'access and enrolment at the primary stage of education have reached near universal levels' (Government of India, 2011b, p. 19), reports suggest that in almost every state, there are many children who have never attended any primary school. These children generally belong to disadvantaged groups, which will be described below. A survey of out-of-school children conducted by the Social and Rural Research Institute of IMRB (SRI-IMRB) revealed that out of a population of 190.5 million children in the age group 6–13 years in 2009, about 8.15 million (4.1 million boys and 4.05 million girls) or 4.28 per cent children were out of school – 4.3 million (53%) of them were in the age group 6–10 years; 3.8 million were in the age group 11–13 years; 7 million (86%) of them lived in rural areas; the remaining 1.1 million lived in urban areas. There has, in fact, been an almost 40 per cent decline in the number of out-of-school children during the years 2005–09 (Ed CIL, 2010). However, in Lewin's view, the number of out-of-school children in India may be much higher, and may range between 10 million and 40 million, depending upon which data source is used for analysis and calculation (Lewin, 2011, p. xxi). The OOSC data produced by the state governments, which is collated through DISE at the national level is, in the opinion of the 15th JRM, an underestimation as compared with the figures produced by the SRI-IMRB. One-fourth of the out-of-school children are those who drop out from schooling along the way while the remaining are those who have never attended any schooling. A careful scrutiny of school attendance and learning achievement records of enrolled children, and the type of school attended by them, including, for example, the aforementioned education centres attended by 16 per cent of children, may well lead to an enhancement of the figures of out-of-school children so far reported.

Children remain out of school due to various deprivations they experience. These may be the result of various social, historical, political, economic and other factors that generally overlap and often operate in combination. An analysis of out-of-school children data based on broad social groupings revealed that 7.67 per cent of out-of school children are Muslim; 5.96 per cent are SCs; 5.6 per cent are STs; and 2.67 per cent belong to Other Backward Classes(OBCs). Similarly, out of a population of 2.89 million (1.52%) of physically and mentally challenged children in the age group 6–13 years, more than a third are out of school (Ed CIL, 2010, pp. 3–5).

However, the extreme condition of poverty of parents is a pervasive reason that affects almost all categories of disadvantaged children and deprives them of opportunities of education and development. It is estimated that families of more than 35 per cent of children in the age group 6–13 years live below the poverty line (BPL). There are different definitions and views as to what poverty actually is. For example, Sen argues that poverty must be seen in terms of deprivation of basic capabilities that provide an individual substantive freedom to lead a life of his or her choice, rather than as lowness of income, which is a standard criteria of identification of poverty, and that income is not the only instrument in generating capabilities. Low access to health care, to sanitary arrangements, or to clean water restrict their substantive freedoms (Sen, 2000, p. 87). Poor access of parents to food, nourishment and health care can adversely affect the educational, physical and psychological development of their children. This has been clearly shown in a study that found that children whose mothers took less healthy food due to poverty had a lower IQ, poorer language abilities, and behavioural and emotional problems (Nomura et al., 2012, p. 784). The severe financial constraint of many families was found to be the most common (38%) reason for the non-enrolment of urban male children in the NSS survey (2007–2008). More generally, 21 per cent of parents could not enrol their children in school due to such constraints; 33 per cent were just not interested in their children's education; and another 22 per cent did not consider education necessary for their children's upbringing and future, and so did not register them in any school. The single most important reason (21.4%) for school dropouts was financial difficulties faced by parents.

Disadvantaged children and their education

A deeper understanding of the problems specific to each category of out-of-school children is necessary for an effective plan to bring them into school and to retain them throughout the elementary education cycle. There are six major categories of disadvantaged children who constitute the bulk of out-of-school children in India. They are girls, children of SCs and STs, Muslims, migrant workers, deprived urban children and children with special needs. Each type has a distinct set of characteristics and specific issues to be addressed and each one may need focused strategies to improve their access, participation and satisfactory completion of elementary education. Gender is a pervasive feature, but it is a separate group as well, and hence girls' education is discussed first among the disadvantaged groups.

Educational opportunities for girls

The significance of girls' education in present-day society can hardly be overemphasized. It is well established that women's education impacts strongly on population growth, home environment and character-building of children during their infancy. A positive education system and experience demands the active involvement of both parents in the education of their children in all its forms – formal, non-formal and informal. This is because both of them are educationally empowered, even if to different degrees. It is estimated that almost three in five households in India are nuclear, with 63 per cent of those in urban areas and 59 per cent in rural areas (IIPS, 2007, p. 23). Education provides parents with the academic equipment to guide and support their children in their overall development. It inculcates in them a desired understanding and appreciation of the value of health, education and character-building of their offspring and of their role and responsibility towards these goals. Lack of education of the mother and father may not only adversely affect the quality of learning and development of their children, but may even restrict chances of their enrolment in school. This was a specific finding in a survey of out-of-school children, which revealed that the foremost reason responsible for keeping children out of school was that parents were not interested in the education of their offspring as they did not find their education to be of any value. Interestingly, in the enrolment of the girl child in school, research has proved that the mother's education mattered more than the father's education (Doraisamy, 2010, p. 311). Or, it may mean that the gap between the educational level of the mother and the father is small (Todd, 1987), at least in rural subsistence communities.

Contemporary society, at least in the more developed parts of India, recognizes the women's role as being much beyond the upbringing of children and home-making. Ideally, it sees and treats them as a valuable human resource of the nation and a partner in nation-building and governance. As rightly observed, educating girls has a catalytic effect on every dimension of economic development, including higher productivity and faster growth (Singh, 2011, p. 226). Consequently, appreciating the significance and need of girls' education, the National Policy on Education 1986 unequivocally declared that education will be used as an agent of change in the status of women and, in order to counterbalance the accumulated deficit of the past, there would be an edge in favour of women. It was affirmed that the national education system will play a positive, interventionist role in the empowerment of women (Government of India, 1986, p. 6). However, six years after the declaration of the policy, the revised Programme of Action (POA) in 1992 still found significant rural–urban disparities among women; rural females remained halfway behind the urban women in literacy, and out of every 100 girls enrolled in class I, only one would survive upto class XII in rural areas as against 14 in urban areas (Government of India, 1992, p. 1).

More recent NSS data (2007–2008) on gross and net attendance ratios shows that initiatives envisaged in the policy documents have lately yielded significant improvements, especially in terms of narrowing the gender disparity as well as the disparity in girls' attendance between rural and urban areas. The NAR in 2007–2008 for females and males in primary classes was 83 per cent and 86 per cent, whereas for upper primary classes, it was 56 per cent and 61 per cent, respectively. Female NAR in urban areas was 84 per cent and 64 per cent at primary and upper primary levels, whereas in rural areas, the corresponding ratios for the two levels were 83 per cent and 54 per cent, respectively. The narrowed gender gap in attendance ratios in both rural and urban areas was also reflected in a high gender parity index[1] of 0.94 at the primary as well as upper primary levels in 2010–2011. The dropout rate at the elementary level not only came down in both genders, but also narrowed between the two. As per the school education statistics compiled by the Ministry of Human Resource Development in 2009–2010, in classes I–V, the girls' dropout rate was 30 per cent, and in classes I–VIII, it was 40 per cent. The corresponding figures for boys were 27 per cent and 44 per cent, respectively (Government of India, 2011a, p. 60). In fact, in 2011–2012, even higher transition rates from the primary to the upper primary level have been reported among girls (85.37%) as compared with boys (84.97%) (MHRD, 2012, p. A2). Although girls' enrolment and attendance rates have improved significantly, the proportion of out-of-school girls (4.71%) to their population in the age group 6–13 years is still higher than that of boys (3.92%). 3.56 million (88%) of the total out-of-school girls are from rural areas and 53 per cent of them are in the age group 6–10 years while the remaining are in the group 11–13 years. This indicates that the bulk of the problem of access, enrolment and attendance among girls lies in rural areas and there too, it is more acute among deprived social groups, namely, SCs, STs, Muslims, migrant workers and children with special needs. In order to bring more girls under the ambit of schools, and address the issue of a gender gap, several initiatives have been taken. The most significant among them is the scheme of Kasturba Gandhi Balika Vidyalaya (KGBV), launched in 2004 to set up residential upper primary schools for girls in rural areas predominantly inhabited by deprived communities. As of now, out of 3,599 sanctioned KGBVs, 3,435 have become operational, with a total enrolment of 0.32 million girls.

Of these enrolled girls, 33 per cent belong to the SC category, 22 per cent to STs, 29 per cent to OBCs, 8 per cent to Muslims and 8 per cent to the BPL category. It is clear that the representation of the SC and ST girls is much higher than their share in population whereas the representation of Muslim girls is still quite low. Similarly, a National Programme for Education of Girls at Elementary Level (NPEGEL) has been launched in educationally backward blocks (subdivisions of districts within states) and already 31,450 schools in 3,122 blocks have been developed into model schools, with additional infrastructure and resources to organize skills-training for girls, bridge courses, and other activities to improve their elementary education. However, notwithstanding the outcomes of these interventions, it seems that the entire approach is focused on the delivery of inputs rather than the adoption of a problem-solving approach to an issue, and equity is not being seen as an integral component of quality. As a result, the real and optimum impact of these interventions is still not seen (MHRD, 2012, p. 17). Reviews have found that NPEGEL is following a fragmented approach to its gender-related activities, which overlaps with other schemes without any cohesive strategy. Furthermore, these activities are not mainstream and therefore not making classroom practices more gender-sensitive, whereas in KGBVs, just to have full enrolment, girls from the categories for whom the institution was started are seldom admitted, which frustrates the very purpose of this intervention (Government of India, 2010, pp. 22–3). Confirming some of these observations of the Review Group, a study on NPEGEL in Jharkhand state found that the benefits of the scheme were not reaching the prime target groups, that is, the SC/STs and minority girls (Kumari and Kumar, 2009, p. 216). A closer norm-based and quality-focused monitoring of these programmes in collaboration with representatives of the target groups may yield more useful information in the future.

Children of scheduled castes and scheduled tribes

The Scheduled Castes and Scheduled Tribes are those communities in India who had been historically excluded from the formal education system and deprived of development opportunities. The former are a feature of the caste system practised in the Hindu feudal society and still influential today. The system is comprised of four hierarchical castes (priests and scholars; soldiers and leaders; craftsmen; general workers), below which are those called *Ati-Shudras* (performing the most menial work) or 'outcastes', consisting of different sub-castes, who for centuries were oppressed and discriminated by the upper castes. The Scheduled Tribes, by contrast, have been deprived of education and development opportunities due to their spatial isolation from the rest of the society, profound cultural differences and marginalization by the dominant, mainstream society.

Despite its long heritage, the scheduling of caste is, however, a relatively recent feature in the long history of Indian civilization (Bagley, 2007, p. 181). Scheduled Castes refer to all those castes which are listed in the Constitution of India for the purposes of extending benefits of affirmative action to them. Dalit (formerly, untouchables, but the practice of being untouchable had been outlawed by Acts of 1955 and 1989) is a term that has been used by these castes to highlight their oppressed status and establish their unique identity and consciousness as the 'other' in Hindu society. The concept owes much to the civil rights pioneer, Dr B. R. Ambedkar, who himself was a dalit. Likewise, all those tribes who were socio-economically marginalized have been listed as Scheduled Tribes in the Constitution. The term *Adivasis* (meaning original inhabitants) is adopted by the tribal communities in order to reclaim their history and unique place in Indian society. Although both SCs and STs have different histories of social and economic deprivation and discrimination and distinct sets of reasons for their educational marginalization, their educational disadvantage presents a common picture and hence a common policy of affirmative action for their educational uplift has been drawn up by the government (Sedwal and Kamat, 2011, p. 87). Movements to abolish the caste system and end discrimination against the lower castes have always proposed education as the primary means to overcome caste-based oppression (Omvedt, 1993 cited in Sedwal and Kamat, 2011). But the nature and history of tribal movements, as Surajit (2002, cited in Sedwal and Kamat, 2011) rightly argues, have been quite different from that of castes. Their basic livelihood needs and the struggle to retain access to forest and natural resources took centre stage in their struggles, while access to formal education remained a secondary issue. Despite different levels of consciousness about education, however, these movements did receive a response from the respective communities. This is evident from their present improved status of education, which is also partly the result of continued affirmative action of the state for their development.

While SCs constitute around 16 per cent of the population of the country, STs are around 8.1 per cent of the population. The former are dispersed all over the country and the latter are concentrated in some states. The present figures of STs and SCs are substantially high (See Table 4.1 below).

Table 4.1 Share of SC and ST children's enrolment in total enrolments and their GERs at primary, upper primary and elementary levels

	Primary level	Upper primary level	Elementary level
SC's enrolment in total enrolments*	20.07%	19.17%	19.81%
GERs of SCs	128%	89%	113%
GERs of SC girls	129%	87%	113%
ST's enrolment in total enrolments**	11.54%	9.43%	10.93%
GERs of STs	139%	83%	119%
GERs of ST girls	137%	79%	116%

*Girls account for more than 48% of these enrolments.
**Girls account for around 48% share.

Source: DISE data 2009–10 cited in NUEPA, 2011.

Such high enrolment figures are encouraging. On the one hand, they present a picture of improved access as well as growing demand and aspiration of these communities for education. On the other hand, as stated above, enrolment ratios in themselves are not conclusively reliable indicators of the real educational progress made. Indeed, there are issues that are indicative of continued educational backwardness of these children, such as rural–urban and gender disparity in enrolment within these groups; high dropout rates (29% and 51% at primary and elementary levels for SCs, and 35% and 58% for STs at the respective levels, which are much higher than the national average); even higher dropout rates for SC/ST girls, especially in rural areas; and poor completion and achievement levels attained by them.

There are various interventions to help the educational disadvantage of SC and ST children, such as KGBV, NPGEL for girls of marginalized groups, Ashram schools for tribal children, pre-matriculation scholarships, hostels and school meals. They have shown some positive results, but not to a satisfactory extent. Equity in education is still being understood in terms of mere equality in access and enrolment. This is despite the fact that there are deeper issues involved in the policy, content, process and management of education that are yet to be fully addressed in order to realize the expected benefits of affirmative action policies. The curriculum and textbooks are not sensitive to the contexts and problems of these communities, and there is little or no representation of the cultural capital of these communities in the curriculum, textbooks and classroom interactions. Students and teachers still maintain a social distance from SC children in classrooms and schools, especially in rural areas, which restricts the SC children's free participation in teaching and learning activities. This was observed by the author during visits to schools in Bihar. As rightly said, the entire emphasis in learning improvement programmes is on making learning joyful and activity-based, rather than taking into account the barrier created by teaching in a different language from the mother tongue of children. This is particularly the case for those from tribal areas and thus is limiting their learning activity and participation and seriously hampering their performance (Jhingran, 2005, p. 8). As far as policies for educational inclusion are concerned, they themselves lack sensitivity to the classroom diversity and needs of the children. They hardly have any mechanism to monitor their implementation by middle and lower administrative echelons and teachers. As a result, Kamat (1985, cited in NCERT, 2005) observed, several decades ago, that educational inclusion policies failed to safeguard the interests of the weak and less influential within the SCs and STs. They remain subject to the influence of the powerful ones who take away most of the benefits accruing from positive discrimination policies (NCERT, 2005). Consequently, the range of social discrimination persisting in schools is only compounding the gross injustice done to SCs and STs in terms of inferior educational provision. Like formal education everywhere, it tends to reproduce the ingrained features of social structure and influence (NCERT, 2005). A more profound and robust policy reorientation is needed, including sensitizing teachers and administrators, redefining curricula, making the context of textbooks more oriented to the realities of the marginalized, teaching about and in tribal languages and monitoring progress on all these fronts.

Educationally backward Muslim children

Muslims account for 13.43 per cent of India's population and constitute the largest religious minority of the country. They are present in almost all parts of the country, and yet the majority of them is concentrated in about 14 states, with a special focus in Uttar Pradesh, where 22 per cent of them reside. Across the whole country, 90 of the 600 odd districts with 20 per cent or more minority population have been declared as Minority Concentration Districts (MCDs). Indian Muslims are not a monolithic entity. They consist of socially stratified groups and exhibit significant class distinctions based on income (Jha and Jhingran, 2005). A majority of them are educationally and economically backward, sometimes even more so than the SCs. A mix of historical, political and other reasons may be held responsible for their continued educational and economic backwardness. These include:

- hostile policies of the colonial rulers against them after 1857;
- partition of India and migration of the Muslim middle class to Pakistan;
- abolition of *zamindari* (landlord) system in Uttar Pradesh;
- spate of communal riots against them after independence (more than 7000 riots between 1960 and 1982 as per Government of India reports) (Ahmad, 1993);
- extreme state of poverty and poor health and nutritional status;
- no affirmative action policies of the government for them;
- administrative and political apathy towards their lot and discriminatory practices followed by administrations;
- attitude of aloofness of the small Muslim middle class and lack of concern for their community;
- lack of initiative and voluntary actions for education.

Decades after independence, in 1980s, a realization began to dawn on the Indian political class that continued backwardness in the education of minority Muslims will seriously deter the development of the entire nation and may blunt its efforts to compete in the globalizing world economy.

Hence, in the National Policy on Education 1986, special provisions were made to support the education of minorities for the first time. However, in succeeding years, not much change was evident. The Sachar Committee, appointed by the Prime Minister in 2006, found that poverty among Muslims was pervasive both in urban and rural areas and that poverty among urban Muslims was even more severe than for SCs and STs in states such as Gujarat, Maharashtra, West Bengal, Chhattisgarh and Uttar Pradesh (Government of India, 2006). Their literacy rate in 2001 was 59.1 per cent as against a national rate of 65.1 per cent. Mean years of schooling of their children aged 7–16 years was 3 years and 4 months, as against a national average of 4 years. This was the lowest among all communities, including SCs and STs, and as many as 25 per cent of Muslim children in the age group 6–14 years were out of school. This was again higher than any other socio-religious category. The proportion of out-of-school Muslim children came down in 2009 to 7.67 per cent of the 24.4 million Muslim children in the age group 6–13 years. Within it, a slightly higher proportion was recorded in rural areas, and the highest proportion (28%) was in Bihar, but this proportion was also much higher than out-of-school SC/ST children (Ed CIL, 2010). The gross enrolment ratio of Muslim children in elementary schools also improved to 13.02 per cent as against their population ratio of 13.43 per cent. This improvement is notable in comparison to the case of SCs and STs, among whom this ratio is almost 25 per cent more than the proportion of their population (NUEPA, 2011). Yet, there are contradictory views. The Sachar Committee observed that despite overall improvement in the educational status, the rate of progress has been the slowest for Muslims and the gap between them and the advanced sections has further widened since independence, and the SCs and STs whose socio-economic position at that time was inferior to Muslims, have now overtaken them (Government of India, 2006, p. 85). This could be due to positive discrimination policies for the education and development of SCs and STs that have been consistently followed since the 1950s. Or, it might be due to an operation of a range of inhibiting factors against Muslim children, such as:

- the communal content of textbooks and prejudiced school ethos;
- perversion of the three language formula in many states;

- resistance to the recognition of minority education institutions;
- perceptions of lack of public security and poverty hindering Muslim families from sending young children, especially girls, to school;
- inapplicability of SC quotas for Muslims though it is applicable to Mazbi Sikhs and neo-Buddhists;
- using Urdu as a marker of Muslim identity rather than as a tool of education.

In addition to policy changes, therefore, what is needed is a change in the mind-set of the middle and higher levels of bureaucracy, that is to say, teachers and educational administrators, through intensive sensitization training and holding them accountable for the education of Muslims. It must be ensured that the different programmes meant for these children are implemented in practice. At the same time, Muslim community elders also have to be pro-active in articulating the demand for quality education of their children as a matter of human rights. Quality education demands inclusive, participatory and unprejudiced classroom processes and a supportive environment that can be organized by teachers duly sensitized to the needs, individualities and sensibilities of minority children (Siddiqui, 2004).

Urban deprived and migratory children

In the past, rural children, particularly girls, attracted more educational interventions from the state and international donor agencies. For many decades, they had been neglected in health care and education. However, children of poor families living in urban slums or of those who migrate from rural areas to cities for shorter or longer periods, within or outside the state, also face the risk of exclusion from education. Their life conditions and chances are as equally vulnerable as those of the rural children. The risk of exclusion may arise due to lack of access to education on account of a lack of schools in their locality. It may also be due to their engagement in an economic activity, with or without parents, to supplement the family income, or due to their household responsibilities, including looking after siblings. The urban poor do not always live in slums. They also live at work sites, at railway stations, in makeshift tents and on pavements. These living conditions, besides depriving their children of education, also expose them to disease, drugs, sex abuse, crime and exploitation. The urban deprived children in India include a wide range of categories – working children, street children, children in slums and resettlement habitations, children of sex workers, children of prisoners, children of construction workers who live within the shells of buildings they construct, children of seasonal migratory labourers and children of those who migrated to cities having been affected by civil strife, violent conflict, social conflicts and natural disasters. However, the Second National Labour Commission (2002) did not consider working children as a sub-category of urban deprived children. In its view, the entire range of out-of-school children in the country must be treated as child labourers or as those who have the potential to become child labourers and they must also include all children working within the family (NCPCR, 2008). While there are no reliable estimates of the urban deprived children by different categories, studies do suggest that their overall number is steadily increasing (Banerji and Surianarain, 2005). According to the SRI-IMRB survey (2009), around 1.1 million children (0.65 million boys and 0.48 million girls) are estimated to be out of school in urban areas. It is further estimated that almost one-third of these children, predominantly boys, are engaged in economic activities and another one-fourth, mainly girls, in household responsibilities including looking after siblings and yet another one-fourth are not doing any work; yet, this group does not go to school for lack of interest in studies. As per one estimate, there are 11.5 million street children in India (Jha and Jhingran, 2005). Seasonal migrant workers' children below 14 years, according to another estimate, are close to 9 million (Smita, 2007; 2011) and one-third of them are living in urban areas. In India, as it may be the same elsewhere in the world as well, there are hierarchies among the poor. The groups we have been discussing here are not only the most deprived and exploited ones, but also quite neglected, and hence deserve special treatment, even at an extra high investment of the governments, if their right to quality education is to be fully ensured.

The government, in collaboration with non-governmental organizations, has been taking action to facilitate the access of these children to formal schools or to alternative venues of education such as education guarantee centres, alternative innovative education centres, back to school camps and bridge course centres. The government has also been supporting *madrasas* (institutions imparting religious education to Muslim children) to provide liberal education as well. Individual state governments have also taken some innovative initiatives to deal with the educational issues of these children. For example, the states of Assam, Gujarat, Rajasthan and Chhattisgarh have developed seasonal hostels, transfer cards and a few other interventions for migratory children. A need is being felt for strengthening of this inter-state coordination for migratory children and to forge such initiatives where these have not yet been taken. Best practices and initiatives, such as the transfer of textbooks between states, and providing progress reports to children from out of the state to enable them to enrol in classes in their home states could be collated and shared (MHRD, 2012). These interventions need to be informed through micro level research in order to maximize the benefits from such initiatives. A study on the impact of bridge course centres in West Bengal reported a mixed result for out-of-school urban children, and recommended better teaching and supervisory inputs to increase the benefit of the programme (Hati, 2011).

Urgent attention also needs to be paid to children who are severely affected by civil strife in some of the eastern and northern states of India, such as Chhattisgarh, Orissa, West Bengal, Jammu and Kashmir, and they need to be insulated from the impact of this strife by enacting laws to prohibit the use of schools by security forces or police, and providing security to children to and from school or, alternatively, rearranging their education in secured locations.

Children with special needs

The education reform perspective demands schools to respond and adapt to the needs of all children, including those suffering from any sensory, cognitive or physical handicap. The Salamanca Conference on Special Needs Education in 1994 urged the world community to 'adopt as a matter of law and policy the principles of inclusive education, enrolling all children in regular schools, unless there are compelling reasons for doing otherwise' (UNESCO, 1994, Salamanca Statement, p. ix). This call has been well responded to in India in the RTE Act 2009, which provides for free and compulsory education of children suffering from disabilities as defined and provided in the Persons with Disabilities (Equal Opportunities, Protection and Full Participation) Act 1996. However, the Act of 1996 does not cover children suffering from cerebral palsy, mental retardation, autism and multiple disabilities. Attempts are being made to include these children within the ambit of the RTE Act 2009. India has made major strides in the education of children with special needs (CWSN), especially after the launch of the *Sarva Shiksha Abhyan* in 2001, which seeks to develop the full potential of each child with any disability by calling for the end of all forms of discrimination and promoting the effective participation of all children. The inclusion of CWSN is emphasized in terms of physical access, social access, quality of access and identification. Mapping and assessment is being carried out for micro planning for inclusion. Around 0.29 million children of ages 6–13 years have been identified as CWSN and about 0.19 million (66%) of them have been brought under the umbrella of formal education (Ed CIL, 2010). Around one-tenth of them are being provided with home-based education through sustained school–community linkages. More than 75 per cent of the CWSN have been provided with assisting devices through collaboration among ministries and institutions. 62 per cent of elementary schools now have barrier-free structures. Some best practices to improve access of CWSN include theme-based activity camps in Orissa organized with parents and peers to facilitate their integration and acceptance; evening camps in Kerala on weekends and holidays to improve the achievement of learners by providing resources, parental guidance, counselling and training to CWSN; and low-cost simulation parks built in Tamil Nadu, especially in rural communities, which provide for play equipment especially for CWSN.

With a view to improving the quality of education for these children, intensive in-service training of regular teachers is being organized to sensitize them to the needs of CWSN, and special educators are being appointed to provide resources to support these children. Peer sensitization through inclusive sports, cultural activities and excursions is done to improve their social access, and parental counselling is carried out to help them teach their children basic survival skills. Despite all these initiatives, a study by the National Council on Educational Research and Training (NCERT) on programmes and practices for CWSN found a continued need for capacity building and managing the attitudinal barriers of teachers for facilitating inclusive education (Julka, 2005a). Another study by NCERT on the use of instructional adaptations by teachers in inclusive classrooms further revealed that due to lack of empowerment, teachers generally preferred using lecture methods for teaching (Julka, 2005b, p. 71). Both studies highlight the major challenge facing the inclusive education of CWSN and the need for effective capacity building and attitudinal changes by teachers in this regard.

Conclusion

Elementary education for all is essential if inequality in society is to be effectively challenged and decreased. Inclusion of all children in education has been attempted by Indian society through implementing policies and strategies to improve access, and lately, by making elementary education a fundamental right of children. Through these attempts, a range of initiatives concerning access, enrolment and completion of the elementary education cycle by children is clearly seen, through which have resulted significant improvements in the schooling of children. However, a major challenge still remains – to improve the quality of education that children acquire while completing schooling, especially those who hail from deprived sections of society. Access alone is not enough. Public Report on Basic Education (PROBE)'s studies in the northern Indian states, first in 1996, and then a decade later, in the same states and areas, reveal that the situation in classrooms and schools which its team visited was not much different from what it had observed 10 years ago, despite several initiatives having been taken by federal and state governments during this period. They were constrained to observe that 'years of schooling and grades completed continue to remain an unreliable guide to what children learn and know' (De et al., 2011, p. 110). The results of the Programme for International Student Assessment (PISA) 2009, a test conducted in 74 countries, including India, not only confirm PROBE's findings, but are also a further concern. The two states that represented India in PISA, Himachal Pradesh and Tamil Nadu, are considered educationally forward. Yet, in reading competence and mathematics, these two states could beat only Kyrgyzstan, whereas in science, the results were even more worrying, as Himachal Pradesh came in the last, after Kyrgyzstan, and Tamil Nadu finished 72nd (Bajpai, 2012).

The broad conclusions reached in PISA tests are born out by the results of evaluation of learning carried out by an NGO, Pratham, and other institutions. Pratham's study on teaching and learning in rural India has shown that most of the children in standards 2–5 were at least two grades below the level of proficiency assumed by the textbooks in language and mathematics (Bhattacharjea et al., 2011). It is because of the poor quality of education in Indian schools that PROBE observed 'the rhetoric of elementary education as a "fundamental right" goes along with a stubborn failure to make the schooling system work' (De et al., 2011, p. 158). This would appear to flag up a bureaucratic deficiency. In practice, the most critical factor that would make the Indian system of education work for all its millions are teachers whose active engagement in non-discriminatory treatment of disadvantaged children become the norm. The government alone needs to take the responsibility to initially prepare and professionally develop these teachers on a continuing basis, besides holding them professionally accountable. Simultaneously, the curricula, pedagogy and assessment procedures need to be flexible. While improving the standards of teaching and learning overall, teachers and schools need to be able to respond to the idiosyncratic needs of every individual pupil.

From the discussion above, it is clear that India, probably more than any other country, has to respond to diverse physical and social contexts. This includes the numerous and diverse learning groups evident among the millions of disadvantaged children. The approach must be truly inclusive, a spirit embodied in the title 'School Without Walls' (Jha, 2002), one of the most inspirational texts arising from the study of disadvantaged children in India.

Questions for reflection

1. What kind of diversities exist in your schools/classrooms? How are they looked at? How are they educationally addressed by teachers, parents, students and school administrators?
2. Do some children face the problem of 'push out' from schools? What are the reasons that lead to such push outs? What steps are taken to address this problem and how effective are these measures?

Note

1 Parity index refers to the ratio of the GER of the lagging subgroup to that of the more favoured subgroup. Thus, a parity index of 1 indicates the two groups have the same NARs; the lower the index gets, the wider the gap of NAR between the favoured and the lagging groups.

Further reading

Banerji, Rukmini and Surianarain, Sharmi (2005). *City Children, City Schools: Challenges of Universalising Elementary Education in Urban India*. New Delhi: Pratham Resource Center/UNESCO.

The book will help readers to have an in-depth view of educational issues of the urban children in large Indian cities and strategies followed to address these issues.

Siddiqui, Mohammad Akhtar (2004). *Empowerment of Muslims through Education*. New Delhi: Institute of Objective Studies.

This book presents a comprehensive fact-based discussion on the educational status and deprivation of children and youth of India's educationally and economically backward Muslim minority community, initiatives taken by the State and the community to educationally empower them and the need and nature of further action to be taken in this regard.

Smita, Prashant Panjiar (2007). *Locked Homes and Empty Schools*. New Delhi: Zubaan.

The publication documents research-based findings on the plight and educational and social deprivation of children of migratory and seasonal labourers and the effectiveness of steps taken to mitigate this problem.

References

Ahmad, A. (1993). *Indian Muslims: Issues in Social and Economic Development*. New Delhi: Khama.

Bagley, C. (2007). 'Dalit Children in India', in G. K. Verma, C. Bagley and M. M. Jha (eds), *International Perspectives on Educational Diversity and Inclusion*. London: Routledge.

Bajpai, K. (2012). Needed Urgently: An Education Revolution. Hyderabad: Times of India. 4 February.

Banerji, R. and Surianarain, S. (eds) (2005). *City Children, City Schools*. New Delhi: Pratham Resource Center/UNESCO.

Bhattacharjea, S., Wadhwa, W. and Banerji, R. (2011). *Inside Primary Schools: A Study of Teaching and Learning in India*. Mumbai: Pratham.

De, A., Khera, R., Samson, M. and Kumar, A. K. S. (2011). *PROBE Revisited: A Report on Elementary Education in India*. New Delhi: Oxford University Press.

Dyer, C. (2000). *Operation Blackboard: Policy Implementation in Indian Primary Education*. Wallingford: Symposium Books.

Doraisamy, M. (2010). 'Enrolment and retention of girls in elementary education in Tamil Naidu', in A. B. L. Srivastava and N. Bala (eds), *Abstracts of Research Studies in Elementary Education (2003-09)*. New Delhi: Educational Consultants in India Limited (Ed CIL), pp. 311–12.

Ed CIL (2010). *All India Survey of Out-of-School Children of 5 and 6-13 years age*. New Delhi: Ed CIL.

Government of India (1986). *National Policy on Education*. New Delhi: Government of India.

—(1992). *Programme of Action 1992*. New Delhi: Government of India.

—(2006). *Social, Economic and Educational Status of the Muslim Community in India*. New Delhi: Ministry of Human Resource Development (MHRD).

—(2009). *Right of Children for Free and Compulsory Education (RCFCE) Act*. New Delhi: Ministry of Law.

—(2010). *Report of the Committee on Implementation of RCFCE Act 2009 and Resultant Revamp of SSA*. New Delhi: MHRD.

—(2011a). *Statistics of School Education-2009-2010 (Provisional)*. New Delhi: MHRD, pp. 4–60.

—(2011b). *Working Group Report on Elementary Education and Literacy: 12th Five Year Plan*. New Delhi: MHRD (Mimeograph).

Goyal, S. (2010). 'Evaluation Study of Para Teachers (Shiksha Mitras)', in A. B. L. Srivastava and N. Bala (eds), *Abstracts of Research Studies in Elementary Education (2003-2009)*. New Delhi: Ed CIL, pp. 325–6.

Hati, K. K. (2011). 'Impact of alternative and innovative education programmes-a study of bridge course centers in Bardhaman District', in *Abstracts of Global Conclave of Young Scholars of Indian Education*. New Delhi: NUEPA.

Gray, H. (2007). 'Diversity, Inclusion and Education', in G. K. Verma, C. R. Bagley and M. M. Jha (eds), *International Perspectives on Educational Diversity and Inclusion*. London: Routledge, pp. 104–12.

International Institute for Population Sciences (IIPS) and Macro International (2007). *National Family Health Survey (NFHS-3), 2005-06, India: Volume I*. Mumbai: International Institute for Population Sciences (IIPS).

Jha, M. M. (2007). 'Barriers to student access and success: Is inclusive education an answer?', in G. K. Verma, C. Bagley, and M. M. Jha (eds), *International Perspectives on Educational Diversity and Inclusion*. London: Routledge, pp. 33–44.

—(2002). *School Without Walls: Inclusive Education for All*. Oxford: Heinemann.

Jhingran, D. (2005). *Language Disadvantage: The Learning Challenge in Primary Education*. New Delhi: APH Publishing.

Julka, A. (2005a). 'A study of programmes and priorities for education of children with special needs in different states', in A. B. L. Srivastava and N. Bala (eds), *Abstracts of Research Studies in Elementary Education (2003-2009)*. New Delhi: Ed CIL.

—(2005b). 'A review of existing instructional adaptations (general & specific) being used in Integrated/ Inclusive classrooms', in A. B. L. Srivastava and N. Bala (eds), *Abstracts of Research Studies in Elementary Education (2003-2009)*. New Delhi: Ed CIL.

Kumar, K. (2010). 'Quality in Education: Competing Concepts'. *Contemporary Education Dialogue* 7(1): 7–18.

Kumari, S. and Kumar, N. (2009). 'Impact study on functioning of NPEGEL program me in Jharkhand', in A. B. L. Srivastava and N. Bala (eds), *Abstracts of Research Studies in Elementary Education (2003-09)*. New Delhi: Ed CIL, pp. 216–17.

Lewin, K. M. (2011). 'Preface' in R. Govinda (ed.), *Who Goes to School: Exploring Exclusion in Indian Schools*. New Delhi: Oxford University Press.

MHRD (2012). *Aide Memoire of 15th Joint Review Mission of SSA*. New Delhi: MHRD (mimeograph).

National Commission for Protection of Child Rights (NCPCR) (2008). *Abolition of Child Labour and Making Education a Reality for Every Child as a Right*. New Delhi: NCPCR.

National Knowledge Commission (2007). *Recommendations on School Education*. Delhi: Government of India.

NCERT (2005). *Position Paper of National Focus Group on Problems of Scheduled Caste and Scheduled Tribe Children*. New Delhi: NCERT.

Nomura, Y., Marks, D. J., Grossman, B., Yoon, M., Loudon, H., Stone, J., Halperin, J. M. (2012). 'Exposure to Gestational Diabetes Mellitus and Low Socioeconomic Status: Effects on Neurocognitive Development and Risk of Attention-Deficit Hyperactivity Disorder in Offspring'. *Archives of Pediatrics and Adolescent Medicine* 166(4): 337–43.

NSSO (2010). *Education in India: 2007-08, Participation and Expenditure, 64th Round*. New Delhi: National Sample Survey Office (NSSO).

NUEPA (2011). *Elementary Education in India-Progress towards UEE, DISE 2009-10*. New Delhi: NUEPA.

Richards, G. (2001). *Gandhi's Philosophy of Education*. New Delhi: Oxford University Press.

Rizvi, F., Engel, L., Rutkowski, D. and Sparks, J. (2007). 'Equality and the politics of globalization in education', in G. K. Verma, C. Bagley and M. M. Jha (eds), *International Perspectives on Educational Diversity and Inclusion*. London: Routledge, pp. 3–20.

Sen, A. (2000). *Development as Freedom*. New Delhi: Oxford University Press.

Sedwal, M. and Kamat, S. (2011). 'Education and social equity in elementary education', in R. Govinda (ed.), *Who Goes to School: Exploring Exclusion in Indian Education*. New Delhi: Oxford University Press, pp. 87–122.

Siddiqui, M. A. (2004). *Empowerment of Muslims through Education*. New Delhi: IOS Publishers.

Singh, G. (2011). 'Elementary Education for Girls in India'. *Journal of Educational Planning and Administration* 25(3): 223–34.

Singh, M. (ed.) (2003). *Maulana Abul Kalam Azad, Profile of a Nationalist*. Delhi: Anamika.

Smita (2007). *Locked Homes and Empty Schools*. New Delhi, Zuban.

—(2011). 'Distress seasonal migration and its impact on children's education', in R. Govinda (ed.), *Who Goes to School: Exploring Exclusion in Indian Education*. New Delhi: Oxford University Press, pp. 315–56.

Todd, E. (1987). *The Causes of Progress: Culture, Authority and Change*. Oxford: Blackwell.

UNESCO (1994). *Salamanca Statement and Framework on Special Needs Education*. Paris: UNESCO.

Vulnerable Children in Ukraine and the Educational Response

Margaryta Danilko and Nadiya Ivanenko

5

Chapter Outline

Context

Ukraine is a major country in Eastern Europe, situated in effect between Russia and the West; most of the other Eastern European countries of the old Soviet bloc have joined the European Union. Its capital, Kyiv, was the focus around the time of the first millennium, with the emergent state of Kiev Rus, which eventually became Russia, with the capital moving to Moscow. Kiev Rus developed at the intersection between the ancient trade routes between China and Europe, and between the Baltic Sea and the Black Sea. Indeed, the considerable length of the Black Sea coast, still enjoyed by Ukraine, including the Crimean peninsula, is one of the most vital economic and geopolitical assets of the country. While within the USSR (1922–1991), Ukraine, with its vast expanse of cultivable steppe lands, became a key component of the Soviet Union, with its vital military asset of the ice-free Black Sea coast. With independence, the significance of these assets diminished drastically, thus adversely affecting the economy of Ukraine, the weakness of which lies behind the massive problem of vulnerable children, with which this chapter is concerned.

The population of Ukraine in 2011 was just over 45 million, with an average life expectancy at birth of 68.5 years. In that year, the number of orphans was officially reckoned to be about 100,000, but that may well be an underestimation since there has been no official count. The incidence of HIV/AIDS is also very high for an industrialized nation, and there could be as many as 250,000 street children.

Official data of the Ministry of Economy of Ukraine indicated that in 2009, 35 per cent of the Ukrainian population was living below the poverty line (according to the official definition of poverty line as 75 per cent of the median daily expenditures per adult). Poverty especially affects families with multiple children, pensioners, and single-parent households. The unequal distribution of social benefits results in a smaller share of assistance being allocated to families in greatest need.

Of Ukraine's more than 6 million children between the ages of 0 and 14 years, approximately 20,000 live in state-run institutions. The main reasons why parents abandon their children are family poverty, unemployment, declining family and moral values, alcoholism, and drug use. Child abandonment can also be seen over the last decade through a growing number of children living and working on the streets. Poverty puts children and young people at risk of being trafficked for the purpose of sexual exploitation and forced labor.

There is no single source of accurate information on the number of homeless children in Ukraine, but informed journalistic estimates place the figure at about 250,000.

In order to reduce, and eventually prevent, child abandonment and to support children living in disadvantaged families, *The Committee on Family Matters, Youth Policy, Sports and Tourism* has approved regulations to help disadvantaged families. During 2005, the government significantly raised social aid for many vulnerable groups. For example, newborn babies and children under the age of three, children in low-income families, the unemployed, retired, disabled, and victims of work-place accidents were all to benefit. However, a State Report about the Situation of Children in Ukraine in 2005 shows that in the current system, not only some groups have privilege over others, but also the income inequality and disparity is further increasing (State Institute of Family and Youth Development, 2006).

Street children

There is no national consensus on the total number of children and young people living or working on the streets of Ukraine, but the number was reported to have increased steadily from 1991 to 2006, with a consequent rise in risk-taking behavior. The number of "street children" who went through the 95 temporary state shelters in 2007 amounted to 11,324 children and young people (Desk Research Report, 2008), but only in 2010 did the Ukrainian authorities publicly recognize the need to reduce the number of homeless children.

The profile of these children and young people appears as follows—the majority are boys, under 18 years, "social" orphans, highly mobile, with low education levels. They leave homes, orphanages, and *internats* (the basic boarding establishments where orphans live and study) as early as the age of 6–7. They then live in cellars, doorways, attics, and sewers. They do not have any access to medical, social, or educational help. Most come from families of alcoholics and drug addicts, but there are also genuine orphans who neither have any expectation of a happy future nor have lived a normal family life. About 70 per cent of homeless children in Ukraine are not parentless; about 40 per cent of them take drugs; close to 60 per cent steal to stay alive; about 80 per cent drink alcohol; over 90 per cent of them have regular sex, starting from the age of six. Begging on the streets and stealing is a way of life for them, as well as various forms of drug and alcohol addiction. Groups of homeless children are structured similar to criminal hierarchies and have criminal connections. Most of those children are from the Carpathian region in the western part of Ukraine, the Donetsk region in the east, and the Crimea in the south. In winter, they go to big cities, and in summer, to the seaside. Forced from their homes and families by poverty, alcoholism, and violence, they eke out an existence by begging, stealing, and working as porters or prostitutes. Having never had, or having lost, their birth certificate, they effectively lose all civil rights and cannot be officially considered citizens of Ukraine. Such is the institutional indifference that street children simply do not exist officially.

Maltreatment and abuse are among the key factors driving children and young people out into the streets and away from home or child care facilities. According to the data of sociological surveys, the most significant causes that force children to run away are beating by parents (30.8% children gave this reason), abuse by parents (28.3%), and peer influences (26.4%) (State Institute of Family and Youth Development, 2006). Another major reason, especially in the western part of the country, is that of parents migrating to other countries in search of employment, especially to Italy, Russia, and Poland. Once on the run, all their human rights are lost, including that of the United Nations Rights of the Child. Only a minority of parents bother, it seems, to try to trace a child who has run away.

About two-thirds of runaways recognize that such a life is not good, but is simply the result of circumstances. After running away, 23.2 per cent of such children live in railway stations, 18.2 per cent "somewhere," 16.4 per cent in garrets, basements, and doorways, and 15.1 per cent on local trains. Some try to work, but most go begging, take money from relatives and friends, and steal. Yet, it is thought that only a tiny minority want to be on the street. Diseases are rampant among these children and the death rate is very high; two-thirds are reckoned to be HIV positive. They use drugs, the most popular being glue and other chemical substances. The majority buy drugs or obtain them from friends, while a minority steal them or are offered to them by parents. The main causes that lead to street children trying drugs are the influence of other people, curiosity, and in a minority, pure idleness. It is striking that these children's knowledge about the consequences of drug use is minimal. Many say that they do not understand the consequences. Others are totally ignorant of them, but do realize that it is possible to come off drugs if treated appropriately.

Trafficking

Trafficking in human beings is a serious issue in Ukraine, which is both a source and a transit country for the trafficking of children for sex work, domestic labor, and marriage. Research shows that of all those engaged in prostitution in the country, 11 per cent are girls aged between 12 and 15, and 20 per cent are aged between 16 and 17 (Trafficking in Persons Report released by Secretary of State Hillary Clinton 16 June 2009). Furthermore, 18 per cent of street children in Ukraine have been victims of sexual violence and sexual exploitation.

The primary destination countries include Turkey, Russia, and Poland. Other major destinations include the Czech Republic, Italy, Israel, Greece, Serbia and Montenegro, the United Kingdom, Lithuania, and Portugal. The number of destination countries used by traffickers has increased, with almost 50 countries serving as destination points throughout Europe and eastward, including China. In 2005, Ukraine increased its law enforcement capacity, proactively investigated trafficking, and strengthened its antitrafficking criminal code. The Government created an AntiTrafficking Department, with over 500 officers assigned throughout Ukraine. It also amended the criminal code to address the full range of trafficking crimes and satisfy the requirements of the *UN Protocol to Prevent, Suppress and Punish Trafficking in Persons, especially Women and Children.* Ukrainian law covers both trafficking for forced labor and sexual exploitation. The government now prohibits all forms of trafficking through Article 149 of its Criminal Code. Penalties range from 3 to 15 years in prison and are commensurate with those for other serious crimes. However, in practice, two-thirds of convicted traffickers received probation instead of prison sentences.

Ukraine's protection efforts remain heavily reliant on international donor funding. While one of the goals of the government's 2007–2010 national antitrafficking plan was to provide assistance to trafficking victims, it has not developed a mechanism for referral or sufficient funding for assistance. Through donor-sponsored programs and some government services, foreign and domestic victims of trafficking in Ukraine receive shelter, medical, psychological, legal, and job placement assistance. The government places child trafficking victims in temporary shelters for children that do not offer specialized services for trafficking victims. Local governments offer sporadic in-kind contributions toward protection of victims, but there is no formal system to proactively identify trafficking victims. While the government has expressed a policy of encouraging victims to participate in investigations or prosecutions through a witness protection program, in practice, it rarely employs this program due to lack of funding or a lack of prosecutors' understanding of it (Trafficking in Persons Report released by Secretary of State Hillary Clinton on 16 June 2009). However, the government, in cooperation with international organizations, has conducted specialized antitrafficking training for investigators, prosecutors, and judges. It has also cooperated with local television channels to broadcast public service announcements and informational programs aimed at raising awareness of human trafficking. This is an example of informal and nonformal education being employed. Government officials speak at public events and in the media to warn citizens about trafficking and to encourage them to be helpful to victims of it. It also encourages inclusion of the topic in the teaching of school and university students.

The Government of Ukraine continues to rely on nongovernmental organizations (NGOs) and international organizations to provide the bulk of victim assistance and protection, of which, more will be discussed below.

It cooperates with international authorities at the port of Odessa and Borispol Airport, Kyiv, but has failed to take steps to establish a credible victim witness program for trafficking victims.

Children in orphanages and internats

About 20 per cent of children without parental care are orphans whose parents have died. The other 80 per cent of the children are social orphans. This means that their parents are alive, but do not take care of their children. Such parents are deprived of their parental rights. The number of orphans and children without parental care doubled during the 1990s and rose to 100,000–120,000 in 2006. The causes of increased child abandonment included family poverty and childbearing by under-age mothers. Children are often removed from families through legal action as a result of family breakdown or other social reasons. In 2009, the number of orphans and children deprived of parental care began to decrease for the first time during the years of Ukraine's independence since 1991. According to the data of the State Service of Youth and Sport of Ukraine, at the beginning of 2011, there were about 98,000 who are either orphans or children abandoned by their parents, or whose parents have been deprived of parental care. During recent years, the number of such children in orphanages and *internats* has been decreasing. In 2011, about 20,000 children were raised in *internats*, while in 2005, the number was about 24,000. In 2010, in Ukraine, there were 78 *internats* with 10,697 orphans, 114 orphanages with 55,154 children aged 3–7, and 48 baby and infant orphanages with 3,704 babies.

During the Soviet period, orphanages and *internats* were the key facilities providing education and accommodation to orphans, with the youngest of them placed in the care of children's houses. Until they reached the age of majority, these children depended on such institutions for lodgings, food, and legal protection. Such institutions failed to provide their wards with adequate and appropriate food, accommodation, and sports facilities; some of them were in a dilapidated condition, without even running water. The main reason for this was inadequate financing by the state (Pryhozhan and Tolstyh, 1990). More importantly, unlike their peers raised in families, children from *internats* are denied the warmth of parental love. In their subsequent adult life, they are unable to resist bad influences or address their problems, even with the aid of official institutions.

Orphans as young as 15 or 16 years old find themselves in a crisis situation—they are forced to leave the relative security of the orphanage. A lifetime of dependence on others creates an inability to make confident and appropriate decisions. They have a severe lack of daily living skills. For most, those problems are aggravated by psychological challenges, such as low self-esteem, lack of communication skills, attachment disorder, and a high level of mistrust of adults. Most fail to continue their education effectively, if at all, or to find and keep jobs. They are unable to locate and maintain housing or build healthy relationships in employment, family, or community contexts. About 10 per cent of orphans commit suicide soon after leaving orphanages (at 15 or 16 years) before their 18th birthday. 60 per cent of girls end up in prostitution and 70 per cent of boys in crime.

Care facilities available to individuals and families

The system of *internats* and orphanages is unable to prepare a child adequately for a self-sufficient life in society at large. In an attempt to address this problem, the Ukrainian government has been paying increasing attention to the development of different family-based forms for the upbringing of orphans and the children deprived of parental care, such as foster families, adoptive families, as well as some alternative care facilities, for example "children villages" (Techniques of Forming and Functioning of Family Type Orphanages, 2003, p. 60).

Adoption

A child can be adopted by a family or an individual. Adoptive children and their parents have legal family relations. An adoptive child has the same legal family rights as the children born into the same family. In 2009, 2,351 Ukrainian children were adopted by the citizens of Ukraine; in 2011 the number was 2108 children.

Foster care

An individual or a family can take from one to four children deprived of parental care or orphans for upbringing in their own family. The child does not lose the status of an orphan or a child deprived of parental care. There are no legal family relations between the foster parents and the children. Foster parents receive money for every child to cover expenses on food, clothes, and other items. Foster parents receive assistance from social workers providing psychological, medical, financial, and legal counseling to family members (Bevz, 2005; Bevz, 2006; Bevz and Pesha, 2001).

They are not usually provided with a house or apartment by the local government. The procedure of placing children in family-type orphanages and foster families, as well as their funding and functioning, are outlined in a special decree /N#564,26.04.2002/ of the cabinet of ministers (State Institute of Family and Youth Development, 2006, p. 66). This determines the status of family-type orphanages and foster families in Ukraine.

In 2009, 2,381 children were taken into foster families; however, in 2011 the number of children taken into foster families was 1,388. Some experts consider this deteriorating situation to be the result of the abolishment of the Ministry for Family, Youth and Sports in 2010, the work of which was focused on placing vulnerable children into families.

Hosting

This is a form of foster care when children live in *internats* and orphanages and spend only weekends and holidays with their foster parents.

Family-type orphanages

This is where a family consisting of a married couple or a single adult takes care of 5–10 orphans or children deprived of parental care. Adults in such families work as institutional instructors and receive salaries, with child support provided by the local government. Importantly, family-type orphanages are usually provided with a house. According to the data of the Ministry for Family, Youth and Sport, in 2010, there were 484 family-type orphanages in Ukraine, where 3,185 children were cared for, and there were 2,931 foster families with 4,934 children overall.

In 2010, 275 million HRV (c£21 million) from the Ukrainian state budget was given for the provision of foster families and family type orphanages. Nevertheless, the number of children taken into this type of orphanages and foster families in 2011 decreased by double in comparison with 2010 and 2009 (in 2009, 2,000 children, while in the first six months of 2011, only 578 children, according to ZN. UA interview of the president's representative on child's rights Lyudmilla Volynets).

Guardianship

Children usually stay in the orphanage or *internat*, but they have official guardians, who are either their relatives or just people who do not have any close relations with them, but wish to care for them.

Kyiv, the capital of Ukraine, has the largest number of foster parents, while family-type orphanages are more numerous in the Crimea and Dnipropetrovsk. Decisions to create foster families or family-type orphanages are the responsibility of the local government, and in particular, their family and youth departments.

Not many people in Ukraine are willing to adopt or foster a child. This is due partly to the fact that the income of the majority of Ukrainian families is still very low. That is why specialists estimate that, for the foreseeable future, orphanages and *internats* will still be the main form of accommodation and education for orphans and children deprived of parental care in the natural family setting.

Responses to the needs of disadvantaged children

State initiatives

The Government of Ukraine has developed a number of policies and programs to benefit children. However, implementation mechanisms and budgetary allocations for these efforts are often inefficient and insufficient. Policy-making is not always well informed due to a lack of data and inadequate analysis. Independence in 1991 afforded opportunities for reform, but as mentioned above, the economic situation of Ukraine inevitably declined considerably. However, in 1996, a Ministry for Family and Youth was established. It became the Ministry of Education and Science, Youth, and Sport at the end of 2010. In the interim, a number of other bodies have been created to help respond to the needs of disadvantaged children and young people. In particular, in April 2001, the Law of Ukraine *On Childhood Protection* was passed. According to this law (articles 10–12), such terms as "orphan," "homeless children," "adoptive family," "family type orphanage," and "foster family" were defined for the first time in Ukrainian legislation. The right of every child, who is in a crisis situation, to live in a family and to have a possibility to be placed into another family for upbringing was fixed (Bevz et al., 2005, pp. 66–7). Then in 2004 came the regulation *About Formation of the State Social Service for Family, Children and Youth* and the regulation *About Measures on Improvement of Social Work with Families, Children and Young People,* as well as *The State Social Service for Family, Children and Young People.* Centers of social services for youth were renamed as the Centers of Social Services for Family, Children, and Youth. Their basic functions are:

a. provision of social services for families, children, and youth by providing them socio-pedagogical, psychological, sociomedical, socioeconomic, legal, and informative services;
b. implementation of social accompaniment for foster families, family-type orphanages, families in difficult life circumstances, social patronage of young people who serve or served their sentences in the form of restriction or imprisonment for a certain term;
c. performance of social prevention work for the prevention of offenses and other negative phenomena in the child's and youth environment, overcoming of the consequences, propaganda of a healthy way of life;
d. implementation of social rehabilitation measures directed to help people in difficult life circumstances (including those who suffered from violence in the family) through renewing broken functions of their bodies, indemnification of restrictions of vital functions and support of optimum physical, psychological, social level for achievement of social adaptation.

Overall, 1,051 centers of social services for family, children, and youth have been created and operate in Ukraine today—27 are regional, 479 at area level, 66 area-affiliated branches, 163 local, 40 districts and towns; and finally, 263 rural and 13 settlement centers.

In January 2005, the parliament of Ukraine passed the law *On Provision of Organization's Legal Conditions for Social Defense of Orphans and Children Deprived of Parental Care.* This law became the background for the development of family-type orphanages for children's education and upbringing. There have been refinements and initiatives subsequently, including in May 2006, with the decision of the cabinet of ministers of Ukraine to approve the state program "*On Prevention of Children's Homelessness and Neglect for 2006-2010.*" The development of family-type forms of upbringing was stressed in it. Nonetheless, up to the year 2012, there has still been no official state statistics on the number of homeless children and children deprived of parental care. The problem is not monitored on a regular basis, the network of social services is not sufficiently developed, and some of them have even been canceled. Although these issues were stated as the main goals of the state program, homeless financing has been dramatically reduced from 20m HRV (c£1.5m) in 2006 to 1.5m HRV (c£100,000) in 2009. In effect, this amounts to virtually no support at all, and so there was a need for international assistance. In 2010, the government of Ukraine, in collaboration with civil society partners, developed a *Road Map to Universal Access for HIV Prevention, Treatment, and Care by 2010*, with technical and advocacy support from UNICEF and its UN partners.

The government has since been working on the introduction of a common mechanism of providing social help to orphans, and children deprived of parental care, according to the principle that money follows the child to guarantee the child's right for an adequate material wellbeing. Every month, each child having this right, no matter whether placed in an orphanage, *internat*, family-type orphanage, foster family, or anywhere else, is supposed to be given directly a definite sum of money. That is in addition to the maintenance such children are provided with, according to the Ukrainian Constitution. For children with special needs, such as the disabled, extra money will be provided according to the norms of Ukrainian legislation. In 2011, the government planned to give 650m HRV (c£50m) for the sanatorium treatment of the disabled, orphans, and other vulnerable children.

Since January 2009, citizens of Ukraine who adopt a child have received social aid of 12,240 HRV (c£1000) from the government (it is given once after the adoption). There is an additional paid holiday for 56 days. Most Ukrainian citizens prefer to adopt very small children, but 90 per cent of the children, who are waiting for the adoption, are older than six. According to the current Ukrainian law regulations, only 30 per cent of orphans and children, deprived of parental care, can be adopted; the other 70 per cent can get their new families in family-type orphanages, foster families, or with the help of the official guardians. In 2009, 12,612 children were given official guardianship and by the end of that year, there were 63,154 children under guardianship in Ukraine. 1,895 children were taken to foster families and family-type orphanages in 2009. By January 2010, 3,185 children were being brought up in 484 family-type orphanages, and 4,934 children were living in 2,931 foster families.

In order to try to prevent child homelessness, the government organization *Services in the Matters of Minors*, together with Ukrainian militia (police), made 23,470 inspections of disadvantaged families, railway stations, computer clubs, and gambling clubs, and found 17, 512 children who had been abandoned by their parents. The number of children who were found for the second time decreased by two per cent in 2010 compared with 2009—another small indication of progress.

Ukraine ratified the UN Convention on the Rights of the Child in 1991 and submitted its first report to the Committee on the Rights of the Child in 1993. But there has been insufficient action taken to develop a monitoring system and evaluate progress in the implementing the Convention. The National Program "Children in Ukraine" was developed within the broad framework of the Convention in 1996. However, the absence of a time-bound and measurable strategy has not allowed for the effective implementation of the Convention as yet. A new national plan of action (NPA) for children is being developed. It is being prepared with the participation of government authorities, civil society, and children themselves, but is constrained by a lack of knowledge, data, and finance. At least the voice of the children themselves is being heard.

NGOs and charities

Many NGOs now work in Ukraine, such as international charity fund "Hope and Homes for Children," youth NGO "Scauts of Kyiv," all-Ukrainian charity fund "Children's World," charity funds "New family," "Children's friends," "Future is in our hands," "Teenager," "Future of orphans," "Development of Ukraine," "Oasis," "Golden Fish," "Boguslav," and others. Some of them provide food, clothing, medical supplies, offer clean accommodation, psychological consultation, summer camps, programs of rehabilitation, job preparation, and legal protection to children and young people. They have been more successful in dealing with systemic problems than have governmental or commercial organizations. Among such successful features are high enthusiasm and personal commitment to serving their "clients," openness to new experiences, and flexibility of strategies of adjustment to client demands.

The main goal of many such organizations is to remove children from the streets, rehabilitate and reintegrate them back into biological or professional families, and help older children lead independent socially acceptable lives. Some of them organize seminars on human rights education for schoolteachers and develop programs to reduce the vulnerability of teenaged orphan youth in Ukraine. Others raise money, operate a telephone hotline for children in crisis situations, deal with housing realities of Ukrainian orphanage leavers, the majority of whom not only have no place to live, but are totally unprepared for independent living outside the orphanage gates.

There are some NGOs who are focused on the problems of Chernobyl children. Chernobyl Children Project USA, established in 1995, nine years after the disaster, is a nonprofit organization that provides medical consultation and evaluation, dental care, clothing, gifts, and social events for the children of the Chernobyl region. In addition, the organization sends medical supplies to the hospitals near their homes. Each year, a medical team from Boston, Massachusetts, visits Russia, Ukraine, and Belarus to choose 100 or so children who have radiation-related diseases. In June, the selected children are flown to Boston for medical and dental care, staying with host families in the area. Almost all of this is provided free of charge to the children's families by the Chernobyl Children Project, thanks to the compassion and generosity of health care providers and businesses in Boston. To date, over 1,200 children have been helped in this way.

The Children of Chernobyl Foundation is one of many worldwide Children of Chernobyl organizations committed to helping the young victims who continue to suffer from the effects of the nuclear disaster. In 2007, 38,000 children from the Chernobyl region were removed from their environment to go abroad for summer respite vacations. Participating countries include Western Europe, the United Kingdom, Canada, Japan, Israel, and many cities within the United States.

Projects and programs

The move toward European integration presents an opportunity for international organizations to enhance their social policy dialogue with the government of Ukraine and to place a child's rights at the forefront of the political agenda and ensure the wellbeing of Ukraine's children.

The United Nations Children's Fund (UNICEF) opened its office in Kyiv in 1997 and has since been working to improve the lives of children and families throughout Ukraine. It implemented a Country Program in 16 regions in cooperation with the government, national civil society, and international organizations over a five-year period, from 2006 to 2010. That program focused on contributing to the reduction of child mortality, improving maternal health, combating HIV/AIDS, protecting the vulnerable, promoting gender equality, empowering women, and developing a global partnership for children. UNICEF has a range of specific programs in action—The *Advocacy, Information and Social Policy Programme, HIV/AIDS, Children and Youth Programme,* the *Child Health and Development Programme, Child Protection Programme, Action on Infant Health Programme, Action on Child Development, Action on Iodine Deficiency Disorders (IDD),* add *Action on Immunization.* The monitoring of child rights and informing policy-making will be assisted through the use of socio-economic analysis based on national data using national and international experience. This is a crucial aid as it acts to combat the lack of capacity in the national system.

In 2006, on the 20th anniversary of the Chernobyl disaster, UNICEF urged the governments of countries still affected by fallout from the radioactive blast to take simple but effective steps to save and improve lives. A lack of iodine in the diets of children living in the contaminated region has made them more susceptible to thyroid cancer and iodine deficiency disorders. Widespread iodine deficiency in the vicinity of Chernobyl is leading to a whole generation of children growing up potentially brain-damaged. These children could be protected through universal salt iodization, which costs almost nothing. UNICEF aims to remind the wider world that children here continue to suffer even though they were born years after the event.

Other projects by international and NGO efforts have been developed during the last decade—the EC project "Strengthening Civil Society," the project "Support to the Development of Social Services for Children and Families at Risk in Ukraine 2007–2010," the information campaign "Every Child Needs a family!," the project "Facilitating Reform of Social Services in Ukraine" (FRSSU), the EU project "Development of a Model of Integrated Social Services for Vulnerable Families and Children in Kyiv oblast," "Hope Now's Orphan/ Children in Need program," "Humanitarian Aid Fund for Children and Vulnerable Groups (AFCV)," USAID programs in Ukraine, "Orphans & Vulnerable Children (OVC)", and "Maternal & Child Health (MCH)".

An all-Ukrainian charity project, "Make Children Happy," has become a regular feature since 2008. It is held during the Christmas and New Year holidays. Famous sportsmen and women, entertainers, and volunteers from more than 30 Ukrainian NGOs and charity organizations take part. In December 2010–January 2011, more than 20,000 orphans and other vulnerable children would receive gifts and take part in different holiday activities.

The implementation of all these projects has enabled the Ukrainian authorities to rely more on Europe's experience in aiding vulnerable families and orphaned children and help to train social workers working with such categories of the population. Much of the work has focused on improving maternal and child health services, reducing micronutrient deficiencies, improving the living conditions inside orphanages and rescue-shelters, providing cottage homes, and encouraging fostering as an alternative to state-run institutions.

Individuals

The role of the individual, both in Ukraine and abroad, is crucial for changing the life of vulnerable children in Ukraine. Some of them have popularized among the Ukrainian people, in general, the idea of orphans living in families, not orphanages; others established and maintained a news section in regional and central newspapers and over the internet, called "Where are you, parents?" to increase the chances of teenage and special-needs orphans of being adopted in Ukraine. Some individuals make an effort to feed unwanted youth; others provide children with shelter, bathing houses, day centers, drug rehabilitation centers, and literacy classes.

Meeting the educational needs of vulnerable children in Ukraine

All the above reforms and initiatives are part of the broad educational response to the problems in question. In this section, we will highlight specific educational responses to the humanitarian needs of children, such as discussed above, and examine the literature on this issue, including in related disciplines such as sociology and psychology. Then, we will examine such responses in the Kirovograd Region of central Ukraine, the City of Kirovograd itself, and Kirovograd State Pedagogical University.

Street living influences a child's physical, intellectual, and psychological state. So, the attitude of most of them to studying is negative. Street children do not go to school, but not because they are necessarily unintelligent. The drug addiction that many of them suffer from degenerates their intellectual capacities. They may even sustain irremediable losses. Many homeless children do not go to school because they are too poor to have clothing that would enable them to fit in socially—a common problem in developing countries. They simply have no time anyway, for they have to earn their living full-time. In any case, the majority of homeless children are not registered for school places or in polyclinics. So, they are not on the list of those who are waiting to get a school-leaving certificate and the passport to be a full citizen of Ukraine. They are nonpersons.

Only 21 per cent of children living in rural areas have access to pre-school education services. Furthermore, the knowledge and skills of parents about child care and development are totally inadequate. More than 600 young children die each year from trauma, accidents, or poisoning due to inadequate parental care. This highlights the fact that appropriate adult education—nonformal and informal—is a vital factor to children being likely to attend schools.

Not only children of alcoholics and poor people run away from their homes. More and more often, children from well-to-do families are also on the streets. This is because they are paid little attention by parents, and substitutes do not exist. Many school societies and clubs have actually disappeared because teachers receive very low salaries, and so are not interested in organizing any extra curricular activities that might extend a helping hand to those who are out of school. Such marginalized and excluded children need that extension of a lifeline to climb out of the vicious circle of life on the streets in the grasp of street adults and other criminal influences. They cannot do it on their own.

Research on vulnerable children

A number of outstanding Ukrainian scholars have worked, and continue to work on the problem of vulnerable children, such as Kapska A. Y., Pesha I. V., Bevz G. M., Komarova N. M., and others. Their research focuses on two main areas:

a. The problems of foster families: In other words, techniques of creation, functioning, and development of adoptive/foster families, the effectiveness of such families, the social situation in such families and in family-type orphanages for children deprived of parental care.
b. The social orphans of Ukraine: In particular, they have examined the system of upbringing of children deprived of parental care, the problems in orphanages and outside, and the state support of vulnerable children.

Students have also examined the problem. Their dissertations focus on the research into educational, psychological, and social problems of children deprived of parental care. They have defended recently in Ukrainian universities. Topics have included the specific character of personality development, problems and behaviors of vulnerable children and the difficulty in bringing up such children who live in *internats*, orphanages, and on the streets. The most characteristic deviations in their behavior have been defined, and preventive methods of their upbringing have been worked out, such as ways of adaptation to life in orphanages and *internats*. Recent examples of such researches in pedagogics, sociology, and psychology are listed in the reference list.

The nonformal and informal education of mass media

Mass media has begun to play an important role in informing the Ukrainian people about the problems of vulnerable children. As recently as 10 years ago, these topics were not even touched upon by Ukrainian newspapers and TV channels. Nowadays, the all-Ukrainian TV studio "Magnolia" offers a special service to find the children who have run away from their homes, *internats*, and orphanages. "Magnolia" throws light on the problems of such children's rights, defends them, and pays much attention to solving their problems and investigating what can be done to help vulnerable children in Ukraine, in general.

The website "Sirotstvy.net" was set up by the TV studio "Magnolia," together with the fund of Renat Akhmetov (a billionaire of Ukraine). Photos of the children who can be adopted and brief information about them are placed on the site.

The all-Ukrainian newspaper "Facty" ("The Facts") has been publishing many articles dealing with the lives of orphans, street children, the problems they face, and the violence they and other children experience from their teachers, educators, and other adults. The number of such articles coming from investigative journalism is increasing.

Regional and local initiatives

Kirovograd region

During 2006–2010, there was a regional program for overcoming the problems of the children deprived of parental care as well as those of homeless children. On 9 December 2010, a regional program under the national plan of realization of the UN Convention on Child's Rights till 2016 was adopted by the regional council.

The project "Reforming educational establishments for orphans and children deprived of parental care" has been ongoing in Kirovograd Region since 2005. As a result, new types of educational establishments for such children have been founded. Nowadays, there are 25 family-type orphanages, 187 foster families in which 497 orphans and children deprived of parental care are brought up. During 2010, 31 foster families and three family-type orphanages were founded and 72 children assigned to them.

The number of children who were taken under guardianship or put into foster families had been 2,045 by January 2011. During the year 2010, 335 children were put in foster families and taken under guardianship in the region; 140 children were adopted, among them 84 by the citizens of Ukraine and 56 by foreigners. There are no data about the number of street children in Kirovograd region as there are no official statistics about this group of children in the whole of Ukraine.

In response to the needs of such children and institutions, the following state social services for the problems of vulnerable children have been established in Kirovograd region:

a. Kirovograd Region Service for the issues pertaining to minors' needs at the regional state administration;
b. Kirovograd City Service for the issues pertaining to minors' needs;
c. Kirovograd State Social service for families, children, and youth;
d. In each of the 21 areas in the Kirovograd region, there is a service for issues pertaining to minors' needs.

The proposals of these services have been taken into consideration while the Kirovograd region development program for 2011–15 was adopted.

Several NGOs and charities are working to defend children's rights in the region, for example, Christian children's fund "Children's Well-Being," a Ukrainian–German charity fund, "Samariter DINST," a charity fund "TAVIFA," and a charity fund "Salvation Army." They have organized four specialized educational establishments for orphans and children deprived of parental care.

Kirovograd City

Within the Kirovograd region, the capital, Kirovograd City, with a population of 255,000, has developed various responses to the needs of its vulnerable children. There is a children's home, an orphanage "Barvinok", an *internat,* and a family-type orphanage. In a children's home, children usually stay till they are three years old. There are special groups for disabled children there. At the age of three, children are taken to the orphanage "Barvinok," where they live till they are 17–18 years old. Most of the children are social orphans. Several of them do not have parents at all or their parents are in prison. They all have the status of children deprived of parental care. Those who are old enough study at a local secondary school (No17) along with the mainstream local children, who have parents and live at home.

In the *internat*, orphans and children deprived of parental care live and study from the first form (6-year-olds) up to the ninth (15–16-year-olds) or eleventh form (17–18-year-olds). Many children who have parents, but who come from very large families, also live and study at the *internat*. The city has 34 foster families and 294 guardianship families.

Kirovograd state pedagogical university

This is located in Kirovograd City and prepares social pedagogues for work in orphanages, *internats*, and different social services working with vulnerable children. Social pedagogy is a rather new specialization and was accredited in 2001. Students who obtain bachelor's degrees can continue their study, taking a graduate course. During their studies, undergraduate and graduate students in psychology and the pedagogics of vulnerable children also do research, writing course papers, and a thesis. They work as volunteers in the orphanage "Barvinok" and in the *internat*, and discuss different problems of the education of marginalized children and their upbringing at the meetings of the university psychology society. Among the subjects of individual theses are graduate theses on social environment as a condition of a person's formation, socialization as a factor of a person's social development, and the formation of communicative competence in future social pedagogues. Undergraduate papers included overcoming of teenagers' addictive behavior in orphanages, development of communicative skills of vulnerable children in orphanages, spheres and directions of a social pedagogue's work, and social pedagogical protection of children and teenagers. While studying at the university, students have the opportunity to undertake various internships in the orphanage and the *internat*, lasting from two to six weeks.

Conclusion

As evidenced above, since the turn of the millennium, there have been a number of achievements in responding to the needs of vulnerable children in Ukraine. The infant mortality rate has been cut by half since 1991. In 2001, the country adopted its first national program on prevention of mother-to-child transmission of HIV. But the transition from a centrally planned economy to a free market has also resulted in an increase in unemployment and social inequality. These are factors that severely affect children, especially since the disintegration of the former state social protection system. The gap between the rich and the poor is widening and the unemployment rate is high, especially in rural areas.

Ukraine has made a number of commitments to improve the wellbeing of children, particularly by signing and ratifying the UN Convention on the Rights of the Child (CRC) in 1991, the Optional Protocol to the UN CRC on the Sale of Children, Child Prostitution and Child Pornography in 2003, the Optional Protocol to the UN CRC on the Involvement of Children in Armed Conflict in 2004, and the UN Convention against Trans-national Organized Crime in February 2004.

Many new regulations dealing with child protection have been developed in Ukraine, some of them reinforced by their international status. Most have been initiated since the turn of the millennium, the majority in the past few years. It will take time for them all to take effect. Meanwhile, a particularly strong challenge remains, which has profound educational dimensions relevant to meeting the needs of the country's disadvantaged children and young people. That is the challenge of HIV/AIDS.

Ukraine is still the country worst affected by HIV/AIDS in Eastern Europe. The number of reported cases has increased in recent years. 80 per cent of the adult population infected with HIV are young people. While the sharing of needles by injecting drug users is the leading cause of transmission, HIV is now spreading fast among the broader young population in general through unprotected sex. As a consequence, increasing numbers of children are born with HIV. The number of infected pregnant women has increased two-fold in the last five years. Most at-risk adolescents are at the core of the HIV epidemic in Ukraine. Little attention has been paid to date to ensure their access to health and counseling services; so overall, the care and treatment for children and families affected by HIV/AIDS is poor. Primary prevention services (to reduce the overall number of children and young people living or working on the streets) are patchy. There are many gaps in services available. Also, governmental organizations are not yet prepared adequately (especially regarding qualified staff) to address the particular and multiple needs of this group and to reach out to them. There are some good practice examples in Ukraine of drop-in centers and psychosocial rehabilitation services run by NGOs or the state, but they are too few.

This is an educational concern as insufficient knowledge about HIV/AIDS contributes to fear, discrimination, and stigmatization. It is not only nonformal adult education that is needed. Clearly, there is a massive educational challenge for those offering both mainstream and special education.

Ukraine is a source country for trafficking in human beings, and this is also an educational challenge. Furthermore, a prevention-oriented juvenile justice system is yet to be established. Consequently, there are no special juvenile courts, specially trained judges, prosecutors, or lawyers to handle children in conflict with the law. Instead, most law offenders are sent to prisons, from where there is little opportunity to reintegrate into society. Little attention is paid to the underlying social factors that lead juveniles into conflict with the law in the first place. This is a major challenge to both the government and civil society as well as an opportunity for research in the universities.

The UN General Assembly proclaimed 2006–2016 the decade of recovery and sustainable development in Chernobyl-affected areas. This means, among other things, providing primary medical services and creating the conditions for healthy and complete child development in these territories, including universal salt iodization, increasing the quality of health care services for mothers and children and their access to them, strengthening the responsible parenthood program, and creating comprehensive service models for families.

All in all, and despite some recent improvements, Ukraine remains in an unenviable position as one of the few countries in the industrialized world with a massive and persistent problem of orphans and other specially disadvantaged children. It will not be in a position to accelerate the modest recent improvements until the dire situation is more profoundly understood in the population at large. That will mean a massive educational effort at all levels, from preschool to university and adult education, and in all its forms—formal, nonformal, and informal.

Questions for reflection

1. What steps do you think would be effective in preventing trafficking of children in Ukraine?
2. What are the most effective care facilities available to vulnerable individuals and families? Why?
3. What is the role of NGOs in educating vulnerable children?

Further reading

UNICEF Country Programme (2011). Available at: *http://www.unicef.org/about/execboard/files/Ukraine_final_approved_2012-2016_20_Oct_2011.pdf.*

The document gives the summary of the situation of children and women in Ukraine, the basic data, the key results and lessons learned from previous cooperation 2006–2011 and the country programme 2012–2016, including preparation process, strategies, relationship to national and international priorities, program components, major partnerships, monitoring, evaluation, and program management.

Ukraine-United Nations Partnership Framework 2012–2016 (2011). Available at: http://www.unicef.org/about/execboard/files/Ukraine_UNDAF_2012-2016.pdf.

The document gives information about four areas in which the United Nations and the Government of Ukraine have agreed to cooperate on: economic growth and poverty reduction, social development, governance, environment and climate change. The reader gets an idea of the general picture and some peculiarities of the current economic, social, political and environmental situation in Ukraine.

Dobrova-Krol, Natasha (2009). *Vulnerable Children in Ukraine: Impact of Institutional Care and HIV on the Development of Preschoolers.* Leiden: Leiden University.

The research paper examines the impact of institutional care and HIV infection on several developmental domains of more than 60 Ukrainian preschoolers. The developmental outcomes of HIV-infected children reared in disadvantaged families are compared with the outcomes of children reared in institutions providing adequate medical and physical care. In search of possible risk and protective factors in the development of these children, individual characteristics and various aspects of the rearing environment are explored.

Help Us Help The Children (HUHTC), a project by the Children of Chornobyl Canadian Fund. Available at: http://www.helpushelpthechildren.ca/index.htm.

HUHTC is a core group of volunteers helping over 30,000 orphans in Ukraine. For more than 12 years, 200 orphanages, hospitals, and rehabilitation centers and clinics have benefited from supplies of medication, food, clothing, and educational toys and materials with a value of over 15 million Canadian dollars.

References

Balakirieva, O. M., Bondar, T. V. and Varban M.Yu. (2000). *Internat Children: About Themselves and Their Life Stories.* Kyiv: Ukrainian Institute of Social Research.

Bevz, G. M. (2005). Adoptive Families: Socio-Psychological Aspects, *Scientific Studios on Social and Political Psychology. Collection of Articles* 9(12): 104–115.

—(2006). *Adoptive Families (Evaluation of Creation, Functioning and Development).* Kyiv: Ukrainian Institute of Social Research.

Bevz, G. M. and Pesha, I. V. (2001). *A Child in an Adoptive Family.* Kyiv: Ukrainian Institute of Social Research.

Bevz, G. M., Boryshevsky, M. Y. and Tarusova, L. I. (2005). *Children of State Care: Problems, Development, Support: Method Guide.* Kyiv: Ukrainian Institute of Social Research.

Cabinet of Ministers of Ukraine (2004a). *About Measures on Improvement of Social Work with Families, Children and Young People.* Regulations No. 1126 of the Cabinet of Ministers of Ukraine, Kyiv.

—(2004b). *About Formation of the State Social Service for Family, Children and Youth.* Regulations No. 1125 of the Cabinet of Ministers of Ukraine, Kyiv.

—(2006). *State Programme On Prevention of Children's Homelessness and Neglect for 2006–2010.* Available at: http://zakon2.rada.gov.ua/laws/show/623-2006-%D0%BF.

Clinton, H. (2009). *Trafficking in Persons Report.* Available at: http://www.state.gov/secretary/rm/2009a/06/124872.htm.

Government of Ukraine (2001). *Law of Ukraine On Childhood Protection.* Available at: http://zakon2.rada.gov.ua/laws/show/2402-14.

—(2005). *Law of Ukraine On Provision of Organization Legal Conditions of Social Defense of Orphans and Children Deprived of Parental Care.* Available at: http://zakon2.rada.gov.ua/laws/show/2342-15.

—(1996). *National Programme Children in Ukraine.* Available at: http://zakon3.rada.gov.ua/laws/show/63/96.

Gubenko, O. V. (2003). Psychological Rehabilitation of the Children who Suffered Exploitation. *Applied Psychology and Social Work* 2–3: 66–77.

Kapska, A. Y. (2005). *Social Work.* Kyiv: Center of Educational Literature.

Kapska, A. Y. and Komarova, N. M. (2003). *Techniques of Forming and Functioning of Family Type Orphanages.* Kyiv: State Institute of Family and Youth Problems.

Levchenko, K. B. and Trubavina, L. M. (2005). *Children's Defense from Violence.* Kyiv: State Social Service.

Parliament of Ukraine (2001). *Criminal Code of Ukraine.* Available at: http://zakon2.rada.gov.ua/laws/show/2341-14.

Pryhozhan, A. M. and Tolstyh, N. I. (1990). *Children without Family: Orphanages, Society Care and Anxiety.* Moscow: Pedagogika.

Shahrai, V. M. (2006). *Social Work Technology.* Kyiv: Center of Educational Literature.

State Institute of Family and Youth Development (2006). *State Report about the Situation of Children in Ukraine in 2005.* Kyiv: State Institute of Family and Youth Development.

Volynets, L. (2011). *In Ukraine Children's Welfare Indices Decrease.* Available at: http://news.dt.ua/SOCIETY/v_ukrayini_za_ostanni_pivtora_roki_pokazniki_dobrobutu_ditey_popovzli_vniz-88609.html.

UNAIDS (2011). *Universal Access to HIV Prevention, Treatment and Care and Support: From Countries to Regions to the High Level Meeting on AIDS and beyond.* Available at: http://www.unaids.org/en/media/unaids/contentassets/documents/document/2011/2011_UA_roadmap_en.pdf.

UNICEF (2011). *Country Programme Document 2012–2016.* Available at: http://www.unicef.org/about/execboard/files/Ukraine_final_approved_2012-2016_20_Oct_2011.pdf.

—(2008). *A Review of the Evidence on HIV/AIDS and most at Risk Adolescents and Young People in Ukraine.* Internal Working Document, UNICEF Ukraine.

United Nations (2000). *UN Protocol to Prevent, Suppress and Punish Trafficking in Persons, especially Women and Children.* Available at: http://ec.europa.eu/anti-trafficking/entity.action?id=ce3a15e0-ed4a-4deb-b218-4cbcb4c7006f.

Zvereva, I. D. (2006). *Social Pedagogics: Theory and Practice.* Kyiv: Center of Educational Literature.

Zvereva, I. D. and Laktionova, G. M. (2004). *Social Work in Ukraine.* Kyiv: Center of Educational Literature.

6 The Use of Sports and College Student Role Models to Enhance Educational Outcomes Among Rural Vietnamese Adolescents

Parker Goyer

Chapter Outline

Introduction

In this chapter, I explain a model for an intervention, Coach for College (CFC), seeking to help youth who are at risk due to living in low-income or rural communities and/or due to membership in stereotyped groups. I highlight the value of intervention during adolescence and during the summers between school years by targeting the psychology of the child. I begin by describing the difficulties that at-risk youth face, and then describe the need for solutions to target three key outcomes societies desire for at-risk youth, namely, greater psychological well-being, greater career success, and higher academic attainment. I then explain the important role that four psychological constructs—goals, motivation, self-efficacy, and self-regulation—play in generating these three longer-term outcomes. I present preliminary evidence for the effectiveness of one possible design for achieving these goals, in the form of an intervention I have developed for rural adolescents in Vietnam. Given that many psychological principles and theories have been formulated in Western contexts, I plan to continue testing the model through future empirical studies in Vietnam and revising it, as appropriate. Though the efficacy of this model will initially be assessed in rural Vietnam, it can potentially be of use to other developing countries that seek low-resource, practical solutions to improve life outcomes among the rural poor, with appropriate adjustments for the cultural context in each locale. In addition, by clarifying the relationships among important psychological constructs and demonstrating which linkages are maintained in different cultural contexts, the evaluation of this intervention can illuminate the aspects of psychological theories that may be universal as well as additional measures that are required to make psychological interventions work in the contexts of developing countries.

Education-related problems facing at-risk youth, focusing on Vietnam

Youth who grow up in impoverished environments are at risk for developing low psychological well-being and for failing to attain the life skills and education necessary for acquiring and succeeding in higher-paying jobs (Hidi and Harackiewicz, 2000). They are also more likely to perform poorly academically and/or prematurely withdraw from school than peers with fewer environmental risk factors (Roeser and Peck, 2003; Peck et al., 2008). Such youth are disadvantaged not due to personal deficits, but due to a lack of material, social, and financial resources in the microsystems that they occupy (Peck et al., 2008; Bronfenbrenner, 1977). Despite the clear environmental challenges, underprivileged youth often internalize low performances or setbacks as evidence of their inadequacy or low ability, and come to devalue the domains in which they occur (Lepper et al., 1986). Although many schools fail to provide students with the level of autonomy, challenge, and relational support they require, schools in low-income communities and/or rural areas particularly struggle in this regard (Pianta and Allen, 2008; Crosnoe, 2001; Eccles et al., 1997).

While all countries face these problems to some degree, they are particularly severe in developing countries, which often possess large rural populations and lower financial resources in general (Bloom and Rosovsky, 2000; Haddad, 2006). Many developing countries are plagued by great disparities between urban and rural areas, which frustrate their attempts to facilitate development. In Vietnam, imbalances in educational attainment between the rich and the poor and between those from urban and rural areas first begin to widen in 6th grade, the first year of lower secondary school, and become most dramatic in 10th grade, the first year of upper secondary school (World Bank, 2008). Dropout is not a major problem in primary school. Approximately 92 per cent of primary school-age children in Vietnam complete 5th grade, and this does not differ sharply by income level or geographic location (Bartholomew, 2009; UNFPA, 2009; World Bank, 2008). Despite nearly universal primary enrollment (Holsinger and Cowell, 2000), Vietnam has difficulty retaining students in the lower (grades 6–9) and upper (grades 10–12) secondary levels. 85.5 per cent of students from rural areas complete 6th grade, compared to 92.9 per cent in urban areas (World Bank, 2008). The gap widens throughout lower secondary school, such that the difference between urban and rural completion of 9th grade is about 11 per cent. By the end of the 10th grade, only 55.2 per cent of rural students remain, compared to 76.8 per cent of urban students. An examination of the completion rates of the poorest students compared to the richest students indicates that poverty and rural residency tend to coincide (World Bank, 2008). According to an earlier World Bank Report in 2005(b), 90 per cent of Vietnam's poor live in rural areas. In 2002, lower secondary enrollment in Vietnam was 85 per cent for the richest fifth of students and a little more than 50 per cent for the poorest fifth (Lan and Jones, 2007).

The core of the problem faced by rural Vietnamese adolescents is a combination of two sub-problems—first, rural youth typically do not stay in education long enough to attain the skills needed for higher-paying jobs, which are typically learned in secondary (Binder, 2009) and especially higher education (Bloom and Rosovsky, 2000; World Bank, 2010). Second, if rural students are fortunate enough to complete high school and take the university entrance exam, the inferior knowledge they have received in their lower quality schools makes it difficult for them to outperform urban students to obtain one of the few places offered (Fong, 2004), much less to meet the requirements of twenty-first-century jobs in an increasingly globalized economy (Nuffic Neso Vietnam, 2009; VietNamNet Bridge, 2011). Because they cannot acquire the education and training needed, rural Vietnamese youth are often forced to take low-paying, physical labor jobs like their parents, which do not meet their needs for competence and autonomy (Goyer, 2010), perpetuating the cycle of rural poverty and undermining both their economic and psychological well-being. Article 29 of the Convention on the Rights of the Child (United Nations, 1989) calls for education that fosters "the development of the child's personality, talents and mental and physical abilities to their fullest potential." Like many countries, Vietnam is currently failing to translate this goal into action (Cohen, 2006).

Appropriateness of social-psychological interventions in the vietnamese context

Thus far, attempts to help the disadvantaged in developing countries have come in the form of broad, abstract goals by international organizations, which are challenging to operationalize (Cohen, 2006). They are also large, structural solutions requiring enormous upfront economic investment that are difficult to carry to fruition, and isolated programs of various kinds whose effectiveness has not been documented through rigorous analysis (Haddad, 2006; World Bank, 2005a). Although negative social and environmental experiences appear to have their most significant impact through the psychological beliefs of the child (Dweck and London, 2004), psychological beliefs have been rarely targeted for intervention in developing countries, as international aid organizations seeking to reduce educational marginalization typically favor an economic or sociological approach (UNESCO, 2007).

Social-psychological interventions may be able to make progress where previous efforts have failed. Because they focus on simple, concrete messages that alter negative psychological beliefs, they generally require minimal resources to implement (Cohen et al., 2006; Hulleman and Harackiewicz, 2009). Moreover, they provide a large return on investment. In many cases, a brief, focused intervention can produce small changes that lead to large effects, such as the reduction of achievement gaps between the advantaged and disadvantaged groups (Cohen et al., 2009; Cohen, 2011; Wilson, 2011; Gehlbach, 2010). Finally, rigorous studies have demonstrated their effectiveness, often through randomized controlled experiments (Wilson, 2011). While social-psychological interventions have primarily been designed and evaluated in Western countries, I hypothesize that they are good candidates for contextual transfer to diverse contexts, such as rural Vietnam, for three primary reasons—the universal difficulties associated with adolescence and life transitions generally (Fox, 1977; Kiell, 1969; Csikszentmihalyi and Larson, 1984), common human psychological needs that occur, regardless of culture (Inglehart et al., 2008; Delle Fave and Massimini, 2005; Dahlsgaard et al., 2005; Cohen, 2006; Welzel and Inglehart, 2010; Ryan and Deci, 2000), and likely similarities in the psychological beliefs of out-groups throughout the world when they are placed in evaluative situations alongside in-groups (Myers, 2009).

Proposal for a targeted intervention

Since summer 2008, a program called Coach for College (CFC) has sought to utilize principles from social psychology to help rural Vietnamese adolescents in one southern province of Vietnam. CFC aims to use sports and older role models as a vehicle to help rural Vietnamese middle school students increase their motivation and ability to take advantage of higher education opportunities via summer camps. In these camps, rural Vietnamese middle school students are given opportunities to learn and apply their knowledge and skills in sports, academics, and psychology from college student mentors in a team-based environment. As a result of the CFC program, students of middle school age are introduced to higher education and its benefits, form strong relationships with positive older role models, develop engagement in, and excitement for, academic subjects, and learn key life skills necessary for the attainment of challenging goals. Through the process of empowering older role models to promote academic and life success among underprivileged rural adolescents, the program also strives to foster the development of the Vietnamese college students and American college student-athletes who participate in the program as coaches, ultimately leading to their transformation into capable leaders equipped to bring about positive change.

The program offers three-week summer camps to adolescent students from all four grades in lower secondary school (6th, 7th, 8th, and 9th) so that students in a given location have a chance to participate each summer and be repeatedly exposed to the principles taught by the camps. In the United States, the separation between disadvantaged and advantaged students seems to originate and become more severe in the summer months (Heyns, 1978; Alexander and Entwisle, 1996). Similarly, interventions designed for low-income, rural Vietnamese youth may also be most beneficial if implemented during this time. Given the strict regulations governing school year education in Vietnam, summer is also the easiest access point for bringing about change in the system, and can serve as a microcosm of what might be effective on a larger scale during the school year. The program is held at a rural middle school, chosen in cooperation with the local government. Holding the program on the grounds of a rural lower secondary school allows positive experiences during the camp to be associated with the school itself. Furthermore, children are given an opportunity to attend either a four-hour morning session or a four-hour afternoon session, the length of time Vietnamese students attend school each day. In addition to being a time period with which students are familiar, it can also serve to demonstrate to government officials the alternative ways in which the school day might be structured to obtain more beneficial outcomes for these youth. Each activity will be described in turn below.

Program activities

The program utilizes five primary activities:

- Sports instruction from highly trained university athletes (sports classes)
- Applied learning modules linked to sports (academic classes)
- Instruction and activities that develop character and life skills (life skills classes)
- Teaching by college student role models
- Team-based organization utilizing principles of organized sports

Sports instruction from highly trained university athletes

Over the course of the three-week camps, youth complete six 45-minute classes in the sports of tennis, soccer, volleyball, and basketball. These classes utilize the sports background and leadership skills of highly trained college athletes to give youth formal instruction on how to play different sports in an organized manner. This instruction is intended to help the youth develop skills and an interest in sports so that they can play them on their own during the academic year, either informally or formally as part of teams. As a universal language and pastime, sport serves as a key mechanism through which to reach those youth who are difficult to access through traditional means; it also serves as a bridge to form strong bonds between people from different cultures and from different socioeconomic backgrounds. Moreover, utilizing sports situations during teaching can make complex math concepts more tangible (Seligman, 2006; Howe, 1999), and beyond that, the analysis of patterns of neighborhood play suggests participation in organized sports provides experience in utilizing complex rules, scoring, and roles, which may be associated with greater math reasoning ability (Entwisle et al., 1994). As students continue to participate in sports classes throughout the program, they will likely develop an increased desire to play sports. Because more frequent sports play is associated with increased self-regulation skills (Holt et al., 2008; Goudas and Giannoudis, 2008; Brunelle et al., 2007), such play can provide further opportunities for youth to practice the executive function skills learned in the program.

Applied learning educational modules linked to sports

These modules focus on the application of sport to selected academic subjects that the students will learn during the upcoming school year. Each student takes six 45-minute classes in four different subjects, entitled "Sports and Health," "Sports and Physics," "Sports and English," and "Sports and Math," each of which can be easily related to sports and may be especially susceptible to summer learning loss if not practiced (Alexander et al., 2007). Each of the six classes in all four modules is based on a lesson from the relevant Vietnamese middle school textbook that students will use in the upcoming school year, and originates from one of four sets of CFC program curricula corresponding to the four different middle school grades. The sports-based academic curriculum (which teaches academic knowledge through sports analogies), along with a learner-centered, constructivist pedagogy, allows youth to see learning as fun and enjoyable. Games and organized sports are natural sources of enjoyment, especially for adolescents (Csikszentmihalyi, 1997). Teaching academic subjects in the context of sports allows youth to engage in applied learning that may trigger a situational interest in these subjects, which over time, may evolve into individual interest that prompts students to study these subjects in more depth on their own (Hidi and Renninger, 2006). This individual interest may even be maintained during the formal school year, when students return to the rote learning methodology typical of Vietnamese schools. Minchew (2002) speculates that sports may contain an emotional intensity that is missing in academic subjects as they are normally taught. Moreover, the connections made between sports (which students are familiar with from the program's sports classes) and academic concepts also help youth learn to understand the abstract, theoretical ideas taught in school in more concrete terms. Along with Heneveld and Craig (1996) and Holsinger and Cowell (2000), the Food and Agricultural Organization (FAO) and the International Institute for Educational Planning (IIEP) contend that contextualized learning in which students are required to "study and resolve real-life problems" (Haddad, 2006, p. 14) is key to encouraging rural children and their families to think of education as relevant to their goals, especially in Vietnam (Lan and Jones, 2007). Finally, by matching the lesson plans with concepts in the textbooks they will use in the upcoming school year, the program can increase the students' ability to do well in school. Repeated exposure to the school curriculum in advance will likely increase the adolescents' chances of performing well in the next school year (Reimers and McGinn, 1997).

Activities that develop character and life skills

The life skills classes utilize strategies proven to be effective through evaluations of social-psychological interventions. Through twelve 45-minute modules held at the beginning of each camp session, the life skills classes instill productive beliefs about ability and the attributions for failure, help students discover and affirm their personal values and strengths, offer exposure to information that gives them the motivation and knowledge needed to develop long-term, academic-related life goals, and provide information about specific self-regulation skills necessary for goal achievement that can often be obtained through participation in sports. Beryl Levinger of the Monterey Institute of International Studies argues that content which addresses "values, processes, and attitudes" (Cohen, 2006, p. 253) in addition to traditional academic instruction is critical for lifting the world's "bottom billion" out of poverty. These skills are especially needed in Vietnam. While Vietnam's rapidly growing economy has a high demand for skilled labor, its education system is only able to produce about half of the skilled workers the government seeks (Nuffic Neso Vietnam, 2009), greatly imperiling the maintenance of its 8.4 per cent GDP growth rate (Overland, 2006). According to a recent newspaper report, as much as 60 per cent of the Vietnamese workforce lacks "life (or soft) skills" (VietNamNet Bridge, 2011), skills that are especially absent in Vietnam's rural population. Deficiencies in Vietnamese educational curricula necessitate as much as a year of retraining once graduates of Vietnamese educational institutions are hired as employees (Nuffic Neso Vietnam, 2009). As a former senior U.S. diplomat in Asia notes, "future [economic] growth [in Vietnam] is highly dependent on a high quality workforce who are better skilled and trained in modern education and with better quality language skills" (Runckel, 2009).

College student role models

All classes in the program are taught by college students, organized into coaching groups of four (two American college students and two Vietnamese college students). Bloom and Rosovsky (2000) suggest a dearth of role models may be a key reason why poor, rural students do not access higher education more often. Teaching and mentoring from college student "coaches" whom youth seek to emulate is likely to be effective in instilling the messages of the program's curriculum, which must be delivered in a credible, compelling way for students to truly internalize them (Cohen, 2011). Using such teachers facilitates positive emotion toward the curriculum being taught (Fredrickson, 2001) and also helps the youth to see the curriculum's messages as convincing since the college students have attained many of the goals the youth themselves seek to accomplish.

The youth can benefit from both kinds of college student coaches. Vietnamese college students from poor, rural communities, like the youths' own, serve as direct role models who demonstrate that attainment of the rural adolescents' desired educational goals is possible within their environment. Csikszentmihalyi (2008) suggests people may be especially effective as positive role models when they are similar in background to underprivileged children. American college athletes offer sports expertise from their years of playing competitive sports, both in sports technique and in the broader life skills that can be learned through sports. Additionally, because the American college athletes provide opportunities for youth to engage in cultural exchange and learn English from native speakers, they serve as a powerful means of attracting hard-to-reach youth to an intervention of this nature. The high coach-to-student ratio in the classes (maximum 4:15) and the in-depth relationship between one coaching group and one of the teams (via the life skills classes) create strong relationships between coaches and individual students, which in many cases last well beyond the three-week camps. College students continue to provide psychological and, in some cases, financial support to the youth during and after the program to help them achieve their goals. Strong relationships with teachers are correlated with increased motivation and performance in school and a lower probability of dropout for adolescents (Cohen, 2006; Juvonen, 2007).

Team-based organization

In each four-hour camp session, youth from a single grade are divided into four teams of 12–15 students and given different colored t-shirts—red, orange, yellow, or green. They complete all parts of the camp with their team. This format creates a small group learning environment that promotes cohesion with peers, a key aspect of "21st-century learning environments" (Partnership for 21st Century Learning, 2009) and can further increase the intrinsic motivation for education. Furthermore, the best parts of the competitive environment of American college sports can be replicated in a foreign setting with little sports infrastructure by creating teams, having participants wear uniforms, encouraging team spirit through slogans and cheers, and providing a forum for teams to compete against other teams. Weekly team-based sports competitions and individual academic and life skills tests give youth opportunities to practice the self-regulation skills they learn about in the life skills classes. The winning teams in each camp have the highest overall score in all three components of the program—sports, academics, and life skills, forcing the middle school students on a given team to rely on each other in all parts of the program in order to succeed.

Outputs

48–60 middle school students participate per four-hour camp session, divided into four teams (96–120 middle school students per camp). 16 "coaches" serve as teachers per three-week camp (eight American college athletes, eight bilingual Vietnamese college students). In one camp, each youth receives 36 hours of instruction in sports and academics (18 hours in each) and nine hours of instruction in life skills. In addition, each adolescent participates in at least 16 hours of sports, academics, and life skills competitions. Every student interacts with 12 of the 16 college student coaches for a total of 9 hours (through the sports and academic classes) and 4 of the college student coaches for 18+ hours (in the sports, academic, and life skills classes, as well as the weekly competitions).

Four three-week camps are held at a given site each summer. Each camp's curriculum is designed for a different middle school grade (6th–9th grade students, aged 11–15). 384–480 children from four middle schools are able to participate in each site each summer, with 96–120 new 6th graders able to enter the program each year in each location. Middle school students can participate up to four times. College students can participate up to two times (the second time as a college director) and can subsequently assume volunteer or staff positions with the program.

Since summer 2008, more than 1,200 Vietnamese students from eight different middle schools have participated in the program, 807 at the original site and 391 at a second site, which was used for the first time in summer 2011. In total, 18 three-week camps have been held over the course of four summer programs. A preliminary study was conducted in February 2010 utilizing a survey to examine the differences between two-time program participants (summer 2008 and 2009), one-time participants (summer 2009), and non-participants on various academic and psychological indicators, with a subset of each group providing in-depth interviews in June 2010. 119 adolescents completed the survey (44 two-time participants, 41 one-time participants, and 34 nonparticipants), providing both close-ended and open-ended responses. 21 of this sample completed semistructured interviews (seven from each group).

Below, the short-term and long-term outcomes expected from the project are described, with some indications found in the preliminary study.

Short term outcomes

Development of long-term, challenging goals

Possible selves

In one life skills class, college students discuss their desired life/career paths as well as a variety of paths youth could choose to pursue within their cultural context. Hearing about the experiences of the American and Vietnamese college students helps youth imagine alternative life/career paths other than the ones with which they are already familiar, broadening the choices available to them and expanding their conceptions of their future selves. They also come to believe that they can be different from others in their community who have low educational attainment and physical labor jobs. When interviewed, students expressed dissatisfaction with the typical life of those in their community who do not achieve higher education. One of the one-time participants explained, "[If I do not obtain higher education], my life will be the same as other people here. They are the people who lack confidence, lack money, and lack knowledge" (one time, 7th grade, 27).[1,2] Once they are aware of pathways that they can pursue that lead to a better future, they develop general aspirations to achieve life and career outcomes they did not think were possible before. Several of the program participants interviewed also explained that the program provided them with knowledge that led them to increase their aspirations. Four program participants said the program made them "want to study to a higher level." Three program participants mentioned that it also helped them "have better preparation to achieve my career goal."

Goal setting self-efficacy

Another life skills class teaches youth how to set personally meaningful, long-term goals, as well as how to make such long-term goals manageable by constructing smaller sub goals. Having been inspired to set challenging goals, youth additionally develop a clear understanding of what is meaningful to them, as well as the importance of developing intrinsic aspirations (such as those that will promote autonomy, competence, or relatedness) rather than extrinsic aspirations. In February 2010, Vietnamese adolescents with greater levels of participation in the program indicated valuing intrinsic aspirations more than extrinsic aspirations. When asked on the survey what goals they had related to education, six program participants indicated they wanted to "have a Master's degree" or "become a PhD." However, these higher level educational aspirations were not mentioned by any nonparticipants. Some mentioned that reaching a higher education level would enable them to "achieve my dream." They described having a better life and a good future without reference to employment or money. Higher education was a goal they had set for themselves. As one student maintained, "I want to complete that level and I think I can do it." As a result of the knowledge they gain regarding how to set goals, youth are able to develop challenging, meaningful personal goals that increase their sense of freedom to make personal choices as well as to imbue their lives with a greater sense of purpose.

Motivation

Extrinsic motivation

Through life skills classes that provide information on the benefits of higher education, youth learn about the connection between education and their personal goals, and how it can allow them to benefit their families and contribute to the improvement of their community and nation. When asked about learning and performance goals, six of the program participants in the survey made their choice because they "[can] help me achieve my goal of completing college." However, none of the nonparticipants made the connection between reaching college and the type of goals pursued in school. When thinking about their country, students with this mindset described the potential of higher education to make the country "become better," "develop," or "become renovated," a view that was more prominent among program participants than nonparticipants. They also understood the dangers of not obtaining education, which served as a motivating force behind their persistence in school. Six students mentioned explicitly that they would have to do a physical job or work as a physical laborer if they did not obtain higher education. A one-time participant explained it this way, "If I do not go to college, my life will be harder; I must do the job with my hands, my leg, my body. It is very hard. I get just a low salary" (one time, 9th grade, 22).

Through the academic classes which teach academic concepts from the Vietnamese school textbooks using tangible examples from sports, youth learn how academics can be applied to real life and help them solve concrete problems they encounter. Making the connection between education and the students' personal goals as well as between education and sports through contextualized learning helps students begin to see education as relevant and valuable to their lives. In the program, youth also develop an increased desire to become more like the college student teachers in the program in order to form deeper relationships with them. An understanding of the value of education, combined with a desire to be like their college student teachers, leads youth to develop increased extrinsic motivation for education. According to one of the two-time participants, "[In the program] I get much knowledge and become more interested in school. The coaches tell me about the benefits of going to college and they encourage me to go to college" (two time, 8th grade, 11).

Intrinsic motivation

Coaches use an interactive teaching methodology to engage students, including asking questions, small group work, role play, and activities/games that illustrate the lesson, teaching practices that make students more excited and interested in learning. Furthermore, when sports are connected with academics, as they are in the CFC academic classes, they can lead to the production of flow experiences during learning, as youth associate their enjoyment of sports with enjoyment of academics. One two-time participant explained the value of this active teaching methodology:

> If I don't achieve my goals, it will be because I am not keen on studying anymore. Because I feel bored with the subjects in school. . .if the teacher does not make the class creative. In the creative class, the teacher incorporates games with the lesson and makes [the students] excited. In the boring class, the teacher just gives a lecture and after that asks [the students] to do the exercises (two time, 7th grade, 14).

Moreover, the concrete nature of sports makes academic concepts more tangible and thus creates an optimally challenging learning environment. Classes are also taught by compelling teachers who make learning fun; youths' affection and enthusiasm toward the college student teachers is translated into affection for what they are teaching. Negative emotions typically associated with academics in Vietnam (anxiety, nervousness) are replaced with positive emotions (excitement, enjoyment), and students develop an increased excitement for and interest in academic subjects. Students may translate this excitement for academics into a love of learning generally, which leads to a thriving orientation (Ford and Smith, 2007) that motivates youth to continue to seek out challenging goals and opportunities throughout life. In comparing the program's academic classes to the school year classes, program participants noted that the program's academic classes made use of games in a beneficial way:

> I prefer studying in [CFC] sports and academic classes because I have fun with games and the lesson. During the school year I have little time to spend on games . . . I think the academics in the program provide me knowledge. It makes me more confident (one time, 9th grade, 19).

The more active methodology also allowed them to feel less nervous and learn more easily, something that was mentioned by three students—"In CFC academics, I can play a lot of games and I feel relaxed. In the school year, I hardly play games and I feel nervous and I cannot take in the knowledge when I feel nervous" (two time, 8th grade, 11). The program's academic classes also seemed to promote conceptual understanding—"I easily take in the knowledge in CFC academics (compared to the school year). Because the [CFC] coaches make me understand better than the teachers" (one time, 7th grade, 16). Moreover, program participants seemed to appreciate connections made between academics and real life—"Academics are different [than in the school year]. In CFC academics I can play and learn and apply what I study into real life. In the school year I just learn without playing. Sports and academics is more helpful because I can learn and see the things to apply in real life" (two time, 7th grade, 14). Even some nonparticipants acknowledged that the degree to which school is interesting "depends on the way the teacher explains the lesson." To make the class interesting, "the teacher may tell them some fun stories" (non, 7th grade, 38). Thus, by increasing their intrinsic desire for learning in a variety of ways, the program seeks to and does strengthen adolescents' motivation for education.

Personal agency beliefs

The program also uses several strategies to increase Vietnamese adolescents' beliefs in their own capabilities. Life skills classes that explain the important steps required to attain higher education help youth understand the critical steps they need to take in order to acquire higher education themselves. Because the coaches have already completed the process, their message is seen as credible by the youth. Separate life skills classes help youth break their long-term, personal goals into smaller, manageable goals that represent specific behaviors youth can control and which help them imagine different pathways to their goals in the event of various obstacles. Youth come to see their goals as optimal challenges rather than as gargantuan, impossible tasks, and develop the belief that they can influence outcomes in their lives, lessening their anxiety about difficult tasks, such as reaching higher education. Other life skills classes provide training in how to process failure in a productive manner so that youth come to see failure as part of the process of achieving challenging goals, rather than as a sign of low ability. As a result of a better understanding of the process for attaining higher education, a perception that their goals can be achieved with enough effort, and a greater internal locus of control, youth are able to persist in working toward their goals even when they encounter obstacles.

The program also affords rural Vietnamese adolescents opportunities to learn about the true stories of poor, rural Vietnamese students who reached college and/or won academic competitions, as well as to directly interact with Vietnamese college students initially from backgrounds like the youths' own. As a result of such in-group role models, adolescents come to believe that they can attain their desired educational and life goals despite the challenges of their environment. In the February 2010 surveys, 25 per cent of two-time participants and 22 per cent of one-time participants said the coaches in the program influenced their choice about the highest level of education they wished to complete. Similar percentages were found for the highest level of education they expected to complete. When asked if there were any way to overcome the obstacles to reaching college, one of the two-time participants said, "I can get the experience from the older students" (two time, 8th grade, 11). Thus, through a better understanding of the process for achieving their goals, a newfound conception of failure, and direct observation of how people from their circumstances have nevertheless earned high achievements, youth develop confidence that they can make substantial progress toward challenging goals if they put forth enough effort. In addition to increasing their confidence in their ability to achieve their future goals, the program also increases adolescents' self-efficacy in the present. Through the sports classes, adolescents gain mastery of skills and techniques in four different sports, some of which they may have never played before. Making improvements in sports allows students to develop confidence and feelings of self-efficacy, which may translate to success in education or in life, especially for girls who did not previously identify with or participate in sports. The program's academic classes help foster adolescents' critical thinking skills, increase their exposure to the school curriculum, and help them better understand abstract concepts presented in their school textbooks. Consequently, youth develop a greater belief in their ability to do well in school. In the interviews, nine of the 14 program participants interviewed mentioned that the program provided them knowledge that prepared them better for the next school year. As one of the one-time participants noted, "The program reminds me the knowledge of the last school year and provides me the new knowledge for the next school year" (one time, 9th grade, 19). When asked whether there were any benefits program participants obtained that nonparticipants did not, nonparticipants said that those who participated in the program gained more knowledge "about the academic subjects they study in the summer" and could "prepare well for the next school year." Self-efficacy developed in sports and academics may, in turn, lead adolescents to have a stronger belief in their ability to master other challenging tasks, such as the attainment of their long-term, personal ambitions.

Self-regulation

Some life skills classes teach skills needed to attain challenging goals through lessons defining key skills and illustrating their use through hands-on activities and real life examples, focusing on emotion regulation, discipline, delayed gratification, flexibility, effective teamwork, and taking initiative. Youth develop a better understanding of what these skills are and how they can be developed.

The weekly sports and academic competitions provide opportunities for youth to practice these skills in real life. Preparation for these assessments requires the exercise of self-discipline, and responding to their results involves practicing emotion regulation. Sports competitions held at the end of each week and an end-of-camp awards ceremony can teach delayed gratification, as youth are required to attend the Monday–Thursday classes to participate in the sports competitions, and are required to do well in the weekly competitions in order to be eligible for team and individual end-of-camp awards.

Thus, through the camp, youth develop positive behavioral habits necessary for the attainment of challenging goals. Moreover, the enjoyable nature of the team-based sports competitions makes youth see sports as exciting and interesting, increasing their interest in sports. As a result, youth may continue to play sports after the camp ends. As students play sports more frequently and/or participate more in the CFC program, they further ingrain and reinforce these positive behavioral habits. The development of such skills is critical to the ultimate attainment of their personal goals. While one-time interventions may be sufficient for changing selected psychological beliefs, such as those associated with stereotype threat (Cohen et al., 2009), repetition of the intervention through multiple opportunities for practice or participation, as demonstrated by Borman and Dowling (2006) and Kwiek et al. (2007), may be necessary to solidify gains in academic knowledge or new behavioral skills.

Long term outcomes

As above, the CFC program helps rural Vietnamese adolescents develop long-term, challenging personal goals, along with the motivation, capability beliefs, and self-regulation skills required to achieve these goals. These are the four psychological constructs that such youth rarely develop in their ordinary environments. The achievement of these outcomes can, in turn, help to address three important problems that afflict Vietnam's young, rural population—the need to increase their psychological well-being, the need to instill life skills that facilitate employment in an increasingly globalized economy, and the need to improve their level of educational attainment.

Increased psychological well-being

By virtue of directly targeting key psychological constructs, the program helps to increase rural Vietnamese youths' psychological well-being over and above the positive emotion they already display. According to Seligman (2011), well-being requires the presence of positive emotion, relationships, engagement, achievement, and meaning. In the program, the coach and team structure allows adolescents to strengthen their relationships with same-age peers and college student role models. The use of games and organized sports as teaching tools fosters engagement and promotes a sense of competence. Competence is further strengthened by instilling productive beliefs about ability and attributions for failure, helping the students affirm their personal values and strengths, and increasing their exposure to the school academic curriculum. Relationships, engagement, and achievement correspond to facets of intrinsic motivation (Ryan and Deci, 2000). The program allows students to obtain meaning by helping them develop long-term, challenging goals, which give a sense of purpose to one's life and serve as an organizing framework for life decisions. Personal goals, capability beliefs, and self-regulation correspond with Ford and Smith's (2007) Thriving with Social Purpose framework. In Ford and Smith's view, enhancement of these three components is key to optimal functioning. Personal goals and self-regulation satisfy the intrinsic need for autonomy, as they afford the youth greater control over their life direction and fulfillment of their desires. Capability beliefs, especially when developed under challenging environmental circumstances, increase the students' sense of competence and desire to approach rather than avoid difficult undertakings in the future. Thus, the CFC program increases rural Vietnamese adolescents' psychological well-being according to both theories.

Development of twenty-first-century life skills

Several facets of the program help students learn and practice life skills—explicit life skills instruction, teaching and coaching by college student mentors, individual academic and life skills tests, team-based sports competitions, and the use of games and organized sports as teaching tools. At a basic level, the development of life skills, such as emotion regulation, self-discipline, delayed gratification, cognitive flexibility, effective teamwork, and taking initiative, can help rural youth be more effective and productive in the jobs available to them in their normal environments, such as farming. The program also helps youth learn how to set goals and persist in achieving them despite obstacles that emerge, fostering a "tenacious personal agency belief pattern" (Ford and Smith, 2007) that can subsequently be utilized to succeed in a wide range of difficult endeavors. These skills are also cited by corporate employers as critical for successful performance in an increasingly globalized economy (Nuffic Neso Vietnam, 2009; Runckel, 2009). Youth who possess such skills will be able to make far greater progress in achieving their desired career goals than their counterparts who do not, and will have a greater ability to acquire and retain reliable employment that adds value to their families, community, and nation. CFC allows for extensive opportunities to develop these skills beyond the initial exposure provided by the first camp. Youth can gain increased behavioral practice with life skills through increased frequency of sports play and/or repeat participation in the program. In the future, CFC will seek to increase the jobs available to rural youth by hiring the best graduates of the program to be local employees who assist in administering the program.

Improved higher education attainment

The program can increase the rural students' persistence in school by increasing their motivation toward school and/or their performance in school. The development of long-term, academic related life goals leads adolescents to have an increased understanding of the value of education, which in turn increases their extrinsic motivation toward school. The small group, collaborative learning with peers fosters an increased sense of belonging at school, and the engaging teaching style and contextualized learning in the academic classes leads to an increased interest in academic subjects. Both school belonging and academic interest are components of intrinsic motivation towards school. Additionally, the program targets improvements in academic performance in multiple ways. Increased self-regulation skills can lead to increased school attendance and an increased effort at school. Effort at school can also be increased through life skills classes that target beliefs about ability and attributions for failure, as an increased concern with mastery rather than avoiding mistakes leads to positive, effort-based strategies in response to failure. Activities that require youth to affirm their personal values and strengths lead to increased self-integrity that is associated with the reduction of exam-related anxiety, a key hindrance with which many Vietnamese students must contend in a highly exam-driven system. Teaching of Vietnamese textbook lessons from the upcoming school year gives youth increased exposure to their school academic curriculum. Increased attendance, effort at school, reduction of exam-related anxiety, and repeated exposure to the school curriculum can each serve to increase the performance in school, an effect that is likely to be especially powerful if two or more occur in combination.

Empirical evidence already indicates progress towards achievement of this long-term outcome. In the February 2010 study, program participants had greater perceived competence in their ability to reach college than nonparticipants. There was also a significant negative association between the level of participation in the program and the dropout rate during the 2009–2010 school year, with the lowest school dropout rate occurring in the two-time participant group. While the program did not have a significant effect on students' perceived competence in school or on students' year-end school grades, there was a trend where greater levels of participation in the program were associated with a lower decline in grades during the middle school years. These results have been corroborated by further analyses in summer 2012. An examination of the cohort of students who entered 6th grade in fall 2008 and were due to finish 9th grade in spring 2012 revealed that, by the end of 9th grade, only 44 per cent of those who did not participate in CFC still remained in school, compared to 75 per cent of those who completed at least one CFC camp. Positive effects were also found for GPA. Those who participated in CFC three and four times consistently performed significantly higher than nonparticipants throughout middle school.

Conclusion

Thus far, no foolproof methods have been found for helping children in the difficult environments that tend to be found in rural parts of developing countries (Haddad, 2006). Even though the effectiveness of many social-psychological interventions has been proven through randomized controlled trials, and some require only minimal inputs to engender large, long-term effects (Gehlbach, 2010), they are often passed over by policymakers in favor of interventions not based on rigorous scientific evaluations and leading to few lasting changes (Wilson, 2011). Greater use of social-psychological interventions that foster empowering mindsets in the face of challenge and which lend themselves easily to scientific assessment could lead to measurable educational progress in regions of the world where it has thus far proven elusive. In a political context such as Vietnam, where government officials are wary of outside influence and extremely concerned with maintaining status quo policies, it is important to take a "foot-in-the-door" approach (Cialdini, 2009) and start change simply and small, by introducing something that is beneficial, but perceived as nonthreatening, such as a summer program. This initial change may serve as a launching pad for more systemic change on both an individual and national level.

The CFC program has several built-in advantages. While the program as yet does not directly address the rural students' inability to afford the fees associated with higher education, it creates a group of American college students committed to supporting the youth participants financially in completing their education and also connects them with Vietnamese college students from similar backgrounds who can explain the strategies their families used to pay for higher education. While good twenty-first-century jobs may continue to prove elusive for rural citizens, the nonprofit organization overseeing the program will seek to hire the best youth participants into volunteer leadership roles and eventually into formal paid staff positions in the future.

Although there is a risk that excitement for education gained during the summer may be lost when youth return to the rigid methodology of the Vietnamese schools, the combination of long-term, academic-related goals, individual interest in academic subjects, and self-regulation skills developed through the program should enable youth to persist as "self-directed learners" (Partnership for 21st Century Skills, 2009) even if they believe their school is boring. In addition, many of the Vietnamese college participants will become teachers in Vietnamese high schools, where they will be able to utilize the active methodology they learned in the program. In time, as government officials observe the effectiveness of the program, they may ask the program to develop teacher guides or workshops so that Vietnamese school teachers can implement these methods in their classes, and may also feel a stronger impetus to reconsider existing systems that limit access to higher education for poor, but qualified students.

By their nature, Vietnamese students are eager, committed, and diligent. Even in rural areas, they can achieve at a high level, if they are shown how school connects to valued goals and if they are given relationships with successful role models who believe in them (Goyer, 2010). However, as the educational system currently stands, substantial human capital is being wasted, endangering Vietnam's economic development as well as the psychological well-being of its people (World Bank, 2010). This wasted human capital includes the rural students who rarely access higher education and who attend poor quality schools, those who fail to pass the university entrance exam each year, and higher education graduates who do not have the skills that today's companies increasingly demand. By involving college students and rural adolescents in a summer program in which they can help each other develop life skills and empowering psychological beliefs, they can become part of a "CFC family," which, if implemented at schools across the country, could become a national movement. Moreover, unlike other national policy solutions, which must be funded mostly internally, the Vietnamese government can potentially draw upon the resources of companies, who would benefit from hiring more skilled workers, and American universities, who are eager for their college athletes to obtain the skills that participation in such a program provides. The prospect of international and public-private partnerships, a students-teaching-students model, and rigorous, scientifically evaluated social-psychological strategies makes the implementation of the "Coach for College" program a promising way to aid Vietnam's rural youth.

Questions for reflection

1. Why do you think finding a solution to curb dropout in rural Vietnam has been so elusive?
2. What considerations should be taken into account when seeking to utilize Western-based psychological principles in intervention work in Vietnam?
3. If an intervention on the whole seems to be working, how can you determine which components of the intervention are responsible for particular outcomes?
4. Besides the dropout rate and GPA, what other metrics could you use to assess the effect of the Coach for College program on Vietnamese youth?

Notes

1 The quotes are from rural Vietnamese adolescents interviewed during June 2010. The first word in parentheses refers to their participation level (non, one, or two). The second word refers to their school grade during the 2009–2010 school year (7th, 8th, or 9th). The third word is a unique number assigned to each person interviewed.

2 All open-ended responses to the surveys and interviews were originally given by the students in Vietnamese and subsequently translated into English.

Further reading

Binder, M. (2009). Why are some low-income countries better at providing secondary education? *Comparative Education Review* 53(4): 513–34.

This article discusses the factors that influence the quality of secondary education in developing countries.

Yeager, D. S. and Walton, G. M. (2011). Social-psychological interventions in education: They're not magic. *Review of Educational Research* 81(2): 267–301.

This article discusses how social-psychological interventions unlock critical psychological barriers that allow positive recursive cycles to develop, boosting confidence, motivation, and educational attainment. It also discusses best practices for designing and scaling them.

World Bank. (2008). *Vietnam: Higher education and skills for growth.* Human Development Department, East Asia and Pacific Region, The World Bank. Retrieved from http://siteresources.worldbank.org.

This report describes factors influencing the access to and quality of higher education in Vietnam, as well as assesses the suitability of Vietnam's higher education graduates for current labor force needs.

Alexander, K. L., Entwisle, D. R. and Olson, L. S. (2007a). Lasting consequences of the summer learning gap. *American Sociological Review* 72: 167–80.

This article discusses the setbacks in learning that occur during the summer months in subjects such as math, science, and language (particularly for low-income students) and why intervention during this time is critical.

References

Alexander, K. L. and Entwisle, D. R. (1996). Schools and children at risk. In A. Booth and J. F. Dunn (eds), *Family school-links: How do they affect educational outcomes?.* Mahwah, NJ: Erlbaum, pp. 67–89.

Alexander, K. L., Entwisle, D. R. and Olson, L. S. (2007). Summer learning and its implications: Insights from the beginning school study. *New Directions for Youth Development* 114: 11–31.

Bartholomew, A. (2009). *Mid-Term Evaluation of the EFA Fast Track Initiative: Country Desk Study, Vietnam.* The World Bank. Retrieved from Education for All Fast Track Initiative website: http://www.camb-ed.com/fasttrackinitiative/.

Binder, M. (2009). Why are some low-income countries better at providing secondary education? *Comparative Education Review* 53(4): 513–34.

Bloom, D. and Rosovsky, H. (2000). *Higher Education in Developing Countries: Peril and Promise.* Washington, D.C.: World Bank.

Borman, G. D. and Dowling, N. M. (2006). Longitudinal achievement effects of multiyear summer school: Evidence from the Teach Baltimore randomized field trial. *Educational Evaluation and Policy Analysis* 28(1): 25–48.

Bronfenbrenner, U. (1977). Toward an experimental ecology of human development. *American Psychologist* 32: 513–31.

Brunelle, J., Danish, S. J. and Forneris, T. (2007). The impact of a sports-based life skill program on adolescent prosocial values. *Applied Developmental Science* 11(1): 43–55.

Cohen, J. E. (2006). Goals of universal basic and secondary education. *Prospects* 36(3): 247–69.

Cohen, G. L. (2011). Social psychology and social change. *Science* 334: 178–9.

Cohen, G. L., Garcia, J., Apfel, N. and Master, A. (2006). Reducing the racial-achievement gap: A social-psychological intervention. *Science* 313: 1307–10.

Cohen, G. L., Garcia, J., Purdie-Vaughns, V., Apfel, N. and Brzustoski, P. (2009). Recursive processes in self-affirmation: Intervening to close the minority achievement gap. *Science* 324: 400–3.

Crosnoe, R. (2001). Academic orientation and parental involvement in education during high school. *Sociology of Education* 74: 210–30.

Csikszentmihalyi, M. (1997). *Finding flow: The Psychology of Engagement with Everyday Life*. New York: Basic Books.

—(2008). *Flow* (3rd ed.). New York: HarperCollins.

Csikszentmihalyi, M. and Larson, R. (1984). *Being Adolescent: Conflict and Growth in the Teenage Years*. New York: Basic Books.

Dahlsgaard, K., Peterson, C. and Seligman, M. E. P. (2005). Shared values: The convergence of valued human strengths across culture and history. *Review of General Psychology* 9(3): 203–13.

Delle Fave, A. and Massimini, F. (2005). The investigation of optimal experience and apathy: Developmental and psychosocial implications. *European Psychologist* 10(4): 264–74.

Dweck, C. S. and London, B. E. (2004). The role of mental representation in social development. *Merrill-Palmer Quarterly* 50: 428–44.

Eccles, J. S., Lord, S. E., Roeser, R. W., Barber, B. L. and Jozefowicz, D. M. H. (1997). The association of school transitions in early adolescence with developmental trajectories during high school. In J. Schulenberg, J. L. Maggs and K. Hurrelmann (eds), *Health risks and developmental transitions during adolescence*. New York: Cambridge University Press, pp. 283–321.

Entwisle, D. R., Alexander, K. L. and Olson, L. S. (1994). The gender gap in math: Its possible origins in neighborhood effects. *American Sociological Review* 59(Dec): 822–38.

Fredrickson, B. L. (2001). The role of positive emotions in positive psychology: The broaden-and-build theory of positive emotions. *American Psychologist* 56: 218–26.

Fong, V. (2004). *Only Hope: Coming of Age under China's One-Child Policy*. Stanford, CA: Stanford University Press.

Ford, M. E. and Smith, P. R. (2007). Thriving with social purpose: an integrative approach to the development of optimal human functioning. *Educational Psychologist* 42(3): 153–71.

Fox, V. (1977). Is adolescence a phenomenon of modern times? *Journal of Psychiatry* 1: 271–90.

Gehlbach, H. (2010). The social side of school: Why teachers need social psychology. *Educational Psychology Review* 22: 349–32.

Goudas, M. and Giannoudis, G. (2008). A team-sports-based life-skills program in a physical education context. *Learning and Instruction* 18(6): 528–36.

Goyer, J. P. (2010). *The Role of Sports-Learning Summer Camps in Influencing Rural Vietnamese Adolescents' Perceptions of their Educational Futures* (Master's thesis). Oxford, UK: University of Oxford.

Haddad, C. (2006). *Addressing Learning needs of Rural People in Asia*. Rome and Paris: Food and Agriculture Organization of the United Nations & International Institute for Educational Planning.

Heneveld, W. and Craig, H. (1996). *Schools Count: World Bank Project Designs and the Quality of Primary Education in Sub-Saharan Africa*. Washington, DC: The World Bank.

Heyns, B. (1978). *Summer Learning and the Effects of Schooling*. New York: Academic.

Hidi, S. and Harackiewicz, J. M. (2000). Motivating the academically unmotivated: A critical issue for the 21st Century. *Review of Educational Research* 70(2): 151–79.

Hidi, S. and Renninger, K. A. (2006). The four-phase model of interest development. *Educational Psychologist* 41: 111–27.

Holsinger, D. B. and Cowell, R. N. (2000). *Positioning Secondary School Education in Developing Countries*. Paris: International Institute for Educational Planning.

Holt, N. L., Tink, L. N., Mandigo, J. L. and Fox, K. R. (2008). Do youth learn life skills through their involvement in high school sport? A case study. *Canadian Journal of Education* 31(2): 281–304.

Howe, M. J. A. (1999). *Genius Explained*. Cambridge: Cambridge University Press.

Hulleman, C. S. and Harackiewicz, J. M. (2009). Promoting interest and performance in high school science classes. *Science* 326: 1410–12.

Inglehart, R., Foa, R., Peterson, C. and Welzel, C. (2008). Development, freedom, and rising happiness: A global perspective (1981-2007). *Perspectives on Psychological Science* 3(4): 264–85.

Juvonen, J. (2007). Reforming middle schools: Focus on continuity, social connectedness, and engagement. *Educational Psychologist* 42(4): 197–208.

Kiell, N. (1969). *The Universal Experience of Adolescence*. London: University of London Press.

Kwiek, N. C., Halpin, M. J., Reiter, J. P., Hoeffler, L. A. and Schwartz-Bloom, R. (2007). Pharmacology in the high school classroom. *Science* 317(5846): 1871–2.

Lan, P. T. and Jones, N. (2007). *Education for all in Vietnam: High Enrolment, but Problems of Quality Remain* (Young Lives Policy Brief 4). Retrieved from http://www.younglives.org.uk.

Lepper, M. R., Ross, L. and Lau, R. L. (1986). Persistence of inaccurate beliefs about the self: Perseverance effects in the classroom. *Journal of Personality and Social Psychology* 50(3): 482–91.

Minchew, S. S. (2002). Teaching character through sports literature. *The Clearing House* 75(3): 137–41.

Myers, D. G. (2009). *Exploring Social Psychology*. New York: McGraw-Hill.

Nuffic Neso Vietnam (2009). *Vietnam's Higher Education: Trends and Strategies*. Ho Chi Minh City, Vietnam: Nuffic Netherlands Education Support Office.

Overland, M. A. (2006). Higher education lags behind the times in Vietnam. *Chronicle of Higher Education* 52(40): A36–9.

Partnership for 21st Century Skills (2009). *P21 framework definitions*. Retrieved from the Partnership for 21st Century Skills website: http://www.21stcenturyskills.org.

Peck, S. C., Roeser, R. W., Zarrett, N. and Eccles, J. S. (2008). Exploring the roles of extracurricular activity quantity and quality in the educational resilience of vulnerable adolescents: Variable- and pattern-centered approaches. *Journal of Social Issues* 64(1): 135–55.

Pianta, R. C. and Allen, J. P. (2008). Building capacity for positive youth development in secondary school classrooms: Changing teachers' interactions with students. In M. Shinn and H. Yoshikawa (eds.), *Toward positive youth development: Transforming schools and community programs*. Oxford: Oxford University Press.

Reimers, F. and McGinn, N. (1997). *Informed dialogue: Using Research to Shape Education Policy around the World*. Westport, CT: Praeger Publishers, pp. 21–39.

Roeser, R. W. and Peck, S. C. (2003). Patterns and pathways of educational achievement across adolescence: A holistic developmental perspective. In W. Damon (Series ed.) and S. C. Peck and

R. W. Roeser (Vol. eds), *New directions for child and adolescent development: Vol. 101. Person-centered approaches to studying human development in context*. San Francisco: Jossey-Bass, pp. 39–62.

Runckel, C. (2009). *The Education System in Vietnam*. Retrieved from http://www.business-in-*asia.com*.

Ryan, R. M. and Deci, E. L. (2000). Self-determination theory and the facilitation of intrinsic motivation, social development, and well-being. *American Psychologist* 55(1): 68–78.

Seligman, M. E. P. (2006). *Learned Optimism: How to Change your Mind and your Life*. 3rd ed. New York: Vintage Books.

—(2011). *Flourish: A Visionary New Understanding of Happiness and Well-Being*. New York: Simon & Schuster.

UNESCO (2007). *EFA Global Monitoring Report 2008: Education for all by 2015, Will We Make it?* Paris: UNESCO and Oxford University Press.

UNFPA Vietnam (2009). *Education in Vietnam: Evidence from the 2009 Census*. New York: United Nations Population Fund. Retrieved from http://vietnam.unfpa.org.

United Nations (1989). *Convention on the Rights of the Child*. Geneva: Office of the United Nations High Commissioner for Human Rights. Retrieved from http://www2.ohchr.org/.

VietNamNet Bridge (2011). Where should Vietnam start education renovation? *VietNamNet Bridge*. Retrieved from *http://english.vietnamnet.vn/en/education/4890/where-should-vietnam-start-education-renovation-.html*.

Welzel, C. and Inglehart, R. (2010). Agency, values, and well-being: A human development model. *Social Indicators Research* 97(1): 43–63.

Wilson, T. (2011). *Redirect: The Surprising New Science of Psychological Change*. New York: Little, Brown, and Company.

World Bank (2005a). *Education in Vietnam: Development history, challenges, and solutions*. Washington, DC: The World Bank. Retrieved from http://siteresources.worldbank.org/.

—(2005b). *Accelerating ural development in Vietnam*. Hanoi, Vietnam: Rural Development and Natural Resources Sector Unit, East Asia and Pacific Region, The World Bank Group in Vietnam. Retrieved from http://siteresources.worldbank.org.

—(2008). *Vietnam: Higher education and skills for growth*. Human Development Department, East Asia and Pacific Region, The World Bank. Retrieved from http://siteresources.worldbank.org.

—(2010). *Stepping up Skills for more Jobs and Higher Productivity*. Washington, DC: The World Bank.

Long-term Social Development through Sports: A Path to Peace

7

Colin Higgs, Carla Thachuk, Hannah Juneau, Racheal Kalaba, and Natalie Brett

Chapter Outline

Long-term social development through sports: Introduction

Sports is a tool, and can be used by governments, communities, and organizations in a number of different ways. Traditionally, sports has been focused on high performance and success or on mass participation for population health. More recently, sports for development and peace has achieved recognition as a cost-effective way to engage children and youth in an activity they love while also using the sports opportunities to undertake youth development initiatives.

Commonwealth Games Canada (CGC) developed the Long-Term Social Development Through Sports model (CGC's LTSDTS), which provides a logical framework for designing sports programs. The framework is based on the known stages of human development and draws heavily on (and is parallel to) the evolving knowledge base around long-term athlete development (LTAD). The CGC's LTSDTS model is moving from being a theory to being the basis for program intervention; it recommends tailoring programs to the development age of the participants, and corresponding the activities and debriefing to achieve specific outcomes for that stage.

This chapter describes the intentional use of sports for social development, outlining some of the existing CGC programming in the Caribbean and Africa, showing the effectiveness of development through sports. The chapter also describes CGC's LTSDTS, the framework for the development, delivery, and evaluation of development-through-sports programs.

Development through sports

The role of sports on children and youth in disadvantaged communities is well established and has been recognized by the United Nations.

> By its very nature, sport is about participation. It is about inclusion and citizenship. Sport brings individuals and communities together. From refugee camps, to slums, to war zones, to violent inner city neighborhoods, sport can improve the daily lives of needy and vulnerable persons. It can make a difference where other means have failed.
>
> Sport provides a forum to learn skills such as discipline, confidence, and leadership, and it teaches core principles such as tolerance, cooperation, respect, and the value of effort. When these positive aspects of sport are emphasized, sport becomes a powerful vehicle through which the United Nations can work towards achieving its goals, in particular the 8 Millennium Development Goals (MDGs). Sport should therefore be seen as an engine for development, not as by-product of it (UN, 2010).

While the importance of sports to disadvantaged children and youth is recognized, the link between sports and creating conditions in which peace can thrive may not be immediately obvious, especially since high-performance sports has been described as "war waged by other means."[1] Inherent in most people's conception of sports, it is defined by high-level competition and the declaration of champions, for celebrating winners, and commiserating with those who are defeated. Traditionally, high-performance sports has been used to advance nationalistic agendas and celebrate the superiority of one nation or ideology over another. This use of sports strives for, and celebrates, high-level accomplishments and has the potential to encourage a "win-at-all-costs" mentality and culture in which the use of performance-enhancing drugs is seen as acceptable. Government interventions in this area are known as *sports development*, which is defined as the planned development of athletes, coaches, teams and ancillary supports, with the goal of improving sports performance and producing elite athletes. *Sports development* focuses on high-performance, competition, results, and the defeat of others; this approach is less conducive to building a culture of peace. For the purpose of this chapter, the culture of peace is a set of values, attitudes, modes of behavior, and ways of life that reject violence and prevent conflicts by tackling their root causes to solve problems through dialogue and negotiation among individuals, groups, and nations (United Nations, 1999). As described above, sports has been recognized by the United Nations as a method of building a culture of peace; as such, the nongovernmental organizations (NGO) sector has developed two approaches to sports—*Sports for All* and *Development through Sports*, which are slowly gaining government support.

The *Sports for All* movement takes a very different approach to sports, focusing on the health and social engagement benefits of taking part in health enhancing physical activity (HEPA). *Sports for All* is a collective term used to describe a range of policies adopted by governments to promote active participation in sports in the community. The origins of the *Sports for All* movement lie with the Council of Europe in the 1960s, but it is now espoused by governments worldwide and by the International Olympic Committee (IOC). Concerns about obesity among young people and about the need to maintain mobility and health among an ageing population have made *Sports for All* a policy of increasing potential importance for community health and well-being (Frawley et al., 2009).

Sports for All is therefore compatible with a culture of peace through its community approach to health promotion, but does not actively pursue a social agenda in which the development of a culture of peace is a clearly identified desirable outcome. Sports for All programs in disadvantaged communities focus on providing social recreation, distraction from pressing problems, and on providing sufficient levels of physical activity to maintain health.

More recently, a third use of sports has emerged internationally. It uses sports as a cost-effective youth development tool, known as *development through sports*. This approach has been embraced by both governments (Commonwealth Heads of Government, 1991; Cooperative Republic of Guyana, 2010) and nongovernmental organizations (Commonwealth Games Canada, 1993). This use of sports to advance a clearly articulated social agenda has become well recognized and has been particularly effective in the fight against HIV/AIDS in sub-Sahara Africa.[2] Kicking AIDS Out, an initiative which CGC supports, is a program that links sports, physical activity, and fundamental movement skills with HIV/AIDS prevention and education. Sports is used to bring people together to participate in games and activities while educating them about practical skills to live a healthy lifestyle. The concept goes beyond HIV and AIDS education and places a strong emphasis on facilitating the development of life skills in youth. James 'George' Nango Otiene, Training and Development Officer, at Kicking AIDS Out Secretariat commented on the importance of sports in his life, growing up in Kenya, and getting involved in sports, which gave him an avenue to avoid crime-related activities and lead to a career in sports:

> *I grew up in Mathare, Kenya, one of the largest, poorest slums in Africa. In the late 1990s, I got involved with a local sport for development NGO called the Mathare Youth Sports Association (MYSA) and began playing football. At the time, I wasn't thinking about learning life skills. I just wanted to be recognized—I had that pride of a youngster who is aspiring to be a football star. If it weren't for sport, I don't think I'd be alive today. Where I grew up, I never considered crime a negative concept because sometimes it was a matter of survival. We were so poor we didn't have a lot of hope (Interview, 2010).*

In the Caribbean, CGC has introduced Bowling Out AIDS (BOA). It is a program similar to Kicking AIDS Out, but uses cricket as the sports. BOA has two goals—improving the sports of cricket and educating participants on the knowledge, attitudes, and behaviors around HIV/AIDS. The program uses coaching cards that are age-specific; each card has the cricket-specific skills a participant should be learning at their age and the teaching skills necessary for the coach to deliver health education at that same age. Theophila Charles, BOA Education Officer, commented on the BOA program and the coaching cards that were created to assist the coaches:

> *It's a good resource, using cricket skills to teach young people about health and HIV/AIDS. It has a lot of useful information. I am able to integrate the subject matter into other subject areas. In Saint Lucia, cricket is introduced to children in primary school. As they grow and learn health and fitness, they will be able to take*

> *a second look at the deeper meaning to support themselves. BOA helps socially and physically. In the school, young people are taught the skills in sport; now they are learning the health aspects as well. They can pass this information to their parents and family members (Interview, 2012).*

To better understand sport's applicability, it is important to differentiate between *sports development* and *development through sports. Sports development* means, as described above, the systematic development of athletes, coaches, teams, and ancillary supports with the explicit intention of improving sports performance, and usually has the production of elite athletes as its major objective. Sports development, therefore, frequently targets athletes, clubs, leagues, and sports systems. *Development through sports*, however, has as its objective the education and social development of children and youth using sports, both as an incentive to attract them to voluntary engagement, and as the medium through which life skills can be taught. In general, the approach used in development through sports has the following characteristics:

a. Use of sports to attract children and youth to voluntary engagement in a program;
b. Playing games/engaging in sports activities for the inherent joy of participation, while including games and activities that have a social learning component; and
c. Debriefing participants after the activity and explicitly linking the lessons learned through the game to life skills knowledge or behaviors.

An example may make this clear. In the southern African country of Lesotho, there is a youth program called Olympafrica Youth Ambassador Program (OYAP), which CGC supports. The program uses well-trained volunteer youth (the ambassadors) to work with orphans and vulnerable children participating in the *Mafube* (rising light/sunrise) programs for orphans and vulnerable children, the *Meraka* program for marginalized "Herd Boys," and the *Girls On The Move* program that engages young women and girls in social development through sports activities. In any one of these *development through sports* programs, the leaders might, for example, play a game with a small group of children. The objective of the game could be for one child to "defend" a small target—say a cone—from being struck by a ball being thrown by other children. The "attacking" children can either throw the ball to another attacker or at the target. The "defending" child therefore needs to constantly move to put themselves between the attacker with the ball and the target, and use their arms and legs to block the ball when thrown at the target. This game is also used for 9–12-year-olds in BOA. There, it is adjusted to have the child defending using a cricket bat while the child attacking is bowling at the wickets being defended.

From a *sports development* perspective, such a game could be used to teach attacking teamwork, defensive positioning, quick foot movements, and anticipation of ball trajectory. When used as a *development through sports* activity, the game would be played in the same way. There would certainly be the same opportunity for the players to learn throwing, catching, and body movement skills, but in addition, there would be a debriefing of the game on some life skills that had been taught beforehand. If the life skill being taught was self-protection against the HIV virus, the group leader could use the game as the basis for discussion with the group about the following points:

1. How the HIV virus can come at you from different directions—from unprotected sex, from contact with other people's blood, and from contaminated needles, razors etc;
2. How the passing of the ball from one attacker can be used as an analogy for the way the virus can be passed from person to person, and the point can be made that you have to protect yourself against everyone (take universal precautions); and
3. How a moment's lack of concentration can let the ball hit the target can be related to the need for constant vigilance against the virus.

In the *development through sports* use of the game, it is the debriefing and social development (life skills) learning that is the key objective; the game is simply the tool to get the message across.

Development of a model for development through sports approach

Commonwealth Games Canada takes the *development through sports* approach and implements programs in Africa and the Caribbean region through its International Development through Sports (IDS) department. The mandate of IDS is to integrate *sports development* and *development through sports* activities in order to build national sports system capacity and promote community and social development throughout the Commonwealth.

Recent evaluations of *development through sports* programs in Africa (Higgs, 2009) have noted a lack of differentiation among programs that correspond to the age of children and youth, and this led to a decision by CGC to explore the possibility of developing a long-term social development-through-sports (CGC's LTSDTS) model. In this section, the process of developing the model and the model itself will be described.

In May 2009, a small workgroup met for two days to create the first draft[3] of CGC's LTSDTS model (see Commonwealth Games Canada, 2009). The model builds on the work already completed in long-term athlete development (sports development). The most advanced model among them is one by Canadian Sport for Life,[4] namely the Canadian Long-Term Athlete Development (LTAD) model (CSC Pacific, 2005). The model has seven stages of athlete development across the human lifespan. The left-hand column in Figure 7.1 shows the seven stages of the Canadian LTAD model, with indications of the typical ages for each stage:

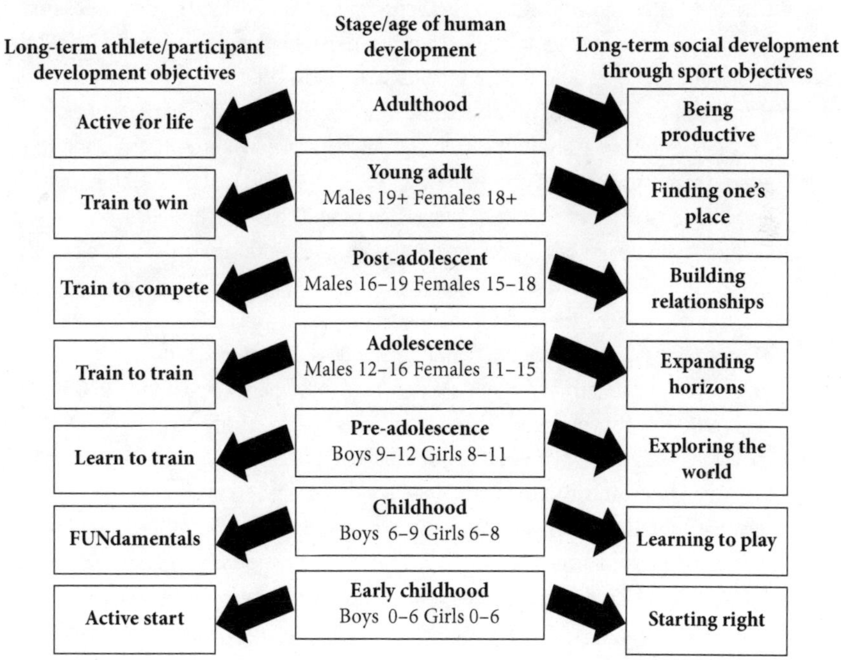

Figure 7.1 Commonwealth games Canada's long-term social development through sport framework

These seven stages were determined based on a review of the human development literature and are well aligned with changes that take place in the human brain and body as it matures. The set-up of the stages was also guided by a question; *what kind of physical activity does a child or youth need to engage in at each age/stage of development to ensure optimum sports participation and/or performance as an adult?* Within LTAD, this question has been answered for the development of strength, endurance, speed, flexibility and sports psychology, optimum training, recovery, and competition. The LTAD model identifies sports and movement specific skills for each stage of physical growth and maturation:

1. *Active start:* the ages from zero to six, for both boys and girls. This is a period of rapid physical and brain growth, and a time during which basic human movements are learned. The end of this state at around six years of age is marked by the age at which the human brain has the greatest number of cell interconnections, and the start of interconnection pruning of unused or underused pathways. It is a time to instill habits of physical activity and a love of movement in children.
2. *FUNdamentals:* From age six to eight in girls, and six to nine in boys. The more rapid physical development of girls is already noticeable during this stage. This is a time during which children need to develop competency in fundamental movement skills, such as running, jumping, catching, throwing, kicking, and striking. This is the optimum time for children to learn these skills, and a child who does not learn them is at risk of being left out of unstructured games played by local groups of children. Children who have learned the skills self-select to play with each other, and those left out miss the increased opportunity to refine their skills that these games provide, and develop a skill deficit that becomes harder and harder to bridge as time passes. Children who do not develop competency in fundamental movement skills are likely to protect themselves psychologically by withdrawing from participation.
3. *Learn to train:* This is the stage from age eight in girls, and nine in boys, to the onset of the child's adolescent growth spurt. It is a time during which the brain is almost fully developed in terms of controlling physical movements, and during which most children have the physical capacity and intellectual ability to learn and refine movement skills to a high level of competence. It is a time for children to become knowledgeable and skillful in culturally appropriate physical and sports skills, and provides a base upon which they can build later in life, either to engage in health promoting physical activity or to pursue higher performance sporting excellence.
4. *Train to train:* This is the period of the youth's adolescent growth spurt, which is generally from age 11–15 in girls and 12–16 in boys. It is a time when the body undergoes enormous physical and psychological change, and a time when development of sports training focuses on "building the engine," the strength, speed, and endurance of the body. It is also a time when sports specialization begins to become more important.

5&6. *Train to compete and train to win:* These two stages are in the realm of high performance sports, and fall within the technical expertise of high performance coaches. The focus is on learning to compete at the highest levels nationally and internationally, and to winning on the world stage. As such, few individuals reach this level of performance.

7. *Active for life:* Whether a person engages in the highest level of international sports or learns the fundamental movement and sports skills during the first three stages of LTAD, there is a need to transition them into being engaged in health-enhancing physical activity for the remainder of their life. Thus, *Active for Life* spans the period in a person's life from the onset of the adolescent growth spurt to old age, and eventually death.

At each stage of development, the physical skills and training required to successfully move to the next stage are articulated, and the model provides a solid framework for the teacher, coach, recreation leader, or health worker to design an effective activity program specific to the stage of development of those in their care.

Conceptually, CGC's LTSDTS model follows the stages of human development established in Canadian Sport for Life's LTAD model and builds on the assumption that the approximate ages from that model were (probably) universal, and therefore equally applicable to the CGC's LTSDTS model. The name of each stage was, however, changed to reflect the social development nature of the model (see the right column in Figure 7.1). In determining this, a guiding question was *what kind of social learning does a child or youth need to engage in at each age/stage of development to ensure optimum participation and performance in society as an adult?* The CGC's LTSDTS framework answers this question by indentifying social development skills that can be taught/learned at each stage of child development—relationship building, communication, self-esteem and empowerment, leadership, team-work, goal-setting, ethical decision making, and conflict resolution. The model aligns their sports and movement skill learning with social skill learning specific to their age and maturation.

Further, the broad objective of each stage of social development was determined by the CGC work group as below:

a. *Starting right:* (ages zero to six for both boys and girls) To create a positive environment for maternal health and the development of good interpersonal relationships between the child and his/her peers and the child and adult caregivers.

b. *Learning to play:* (ages six to eight for girls, six to nine for boys) To help children learn to work and play as part of a group, to learn rule-based activities and the consequences of breaking the rules, and finally, develop competence-based self-esteem.
c. *Exploring the world:* (ages 8–11 for girls, 9–12 for boys) Learning respect for self and for partners, opponents, and officials while developing social responsibility and learning to live in, and be part of, the broader community.
d. *Expanding horizons:* (ages 11–15 for girls, 12–16 for boys) Developing respect for one's self and for one's body; making good decisions and understanding safe and unsafe behavior in the use of drugs and alcohol, and engagement in sexual activity.
e. *Building relationships:* (ages 15–18 for females, 16–19 for males) Understanding and building stable relationships, sexual activity, safe sex, drug and alcohol avoidance/harm reduction strategies, and employment planning.
f. *Finding one's place:* (ages 18 and above for females, 19 and above for males) Developing adult relationships, enhancing employment skills, becoming a role model, and learning about leadership positions within the community.
g. *Being productive:* (any adult age) Becoming a leader in the community, helping and training others.

Having established the broad social objective at each stage of development, CGC addressed which specific areas of social development were of greatest importance to the chances of long-term success of a child/youth as he or she move into adulthood. This was a difficult task as there was never complete consensus; the following list of focus areas was one with which all of the participants (comprised of four experts from CGC) in the discussion could agree, albeit with some reservations.

They are:

a. Relationships: How to develop healthy relationships with parents, caregivers, peers, and other members of the community. How to develop positive sexual relationships at an appropriate age, and how to protect yourself and partners.
b. Communication skills: How the individual communicated verbally (speaking and listening), in text (reading and writing), and through body language with those around him/her, including caregivers, peers, leaders and followers.
c. Self-esteem and empowerment: Developing a positive self-image, positive self-esteem and a feeling of control over one's destiny—a feeling of empowerment.
d. Leadership, teamwork, and goal-setting: Learning to work as part of a team, as a leader and follower, working alone, and with others to develop personal and group goals.

e. Making ethical decisions: The decision-making process, analyzing the consequences of decisions, making good decisions, making ethical decisions, learning techniques for protection against peer (and other negative) pressures.

After receiving feedback on the original five focus areas in the framework from other professionals working in the field of *development through sports*, two additional focus areas were added:

f. Conflict reduction/resolution: Techniques for conflict reduction/transformation, for developing empathy, and for intervention techniques.
g. Sustainability: Understanding the need for environmental stewardship and the development of skills to enable economic independence in adulthood.

This produced a *7 x 7* matrix of seven stages of development by seven social development focus areas in the development of a well-balanced adult. Within each cell—that is, at a specific stage of development within a social development area—the key social development objectives for the child/youth were identified, as were any critical knowledge skills or learnings required by a leader working with youth at that stage of development.

This matrix must be considered a work-in-progress rather than a finished product. CGC has started the process of sharing this matrix with interested colleagues and will be incorporating the feedback received into more refined versions of the model. Two types of colleagues are currently involved in the review process—academics working in the area of development through sports and practitioners working on the frontlines of development through sports programs in Africa and the Caribbean.

Long-term social development through sports provides a logical framework for program design, taking into account the known developmental stages through which children and youth pass. It suggests the need to explicitly tailor intervention programs to the stage of development of the participants, and to tailor activities and debriefings to achieve specific outcomes. It is, however, in its infancy. CGC's LTSDTS has moved from being a theory to being the basis for program interventions. It is starting to be used in the design delivery of evaluation of *development through sports* programs (see Commonwealth Games Canada, 2009), and over the next few years, it will start to provide valuable evidence to enable us to evaluate its effectiveness.

Sports and the development of a culture of peace

As stated earlier, *development through sports* actively pursues a social agenda in which the development of a culture of peace is a clearly identified desirable outcome. Therefore, how sports can contribute to a culture of peace will be discussed in this section. As explained by the Peace and Sport organization, who, through structured teaching of sports and its values, educates people and encourages a peace culture to emerge:

> Peace is not merely a state of absence of war: peace is taught, learned and transmitted.
>
> Fair play, morality, trust in others, teamwork, social integration, listening, discipline and talent: sport is a universal language in which one rule unites everyone. Much more than a game, it is a tool for dialogue, brotherhood and respect that transcends political, social, racial, ethnical and religious differences that are often at the heart of conflicts in this world (Peace and Sport, 2010).

In promoting a culture of peace, it is crucial to teach conflict reduction/resolution skills; the innate competitiveness that sports creates can generate conflict in which *development through sports* programs can channel the practical application and inclusion of conflict reduction/conflict resolution skills. These specific conflict resolution skills, progressively developed in youth as they pass through each stage of development, are significantly enhanced and supported through the other skills they learn. In CGC's Kicking AIDS Out program, soccer is used to teach HIV/AIDS prevention and incorporates social development skills into some of its activities. Hot Ball is used to teach conflict resolution and decision-making skills; one participant starts with the ball and acts as if he/she is setting the ball on fire, then passes it to another participant in the circle; once the ball leaves the circle, the last person to touch it restarts the process. Once the activity is complete, the coach debriefs by discussing the following points with the participants:

- What are the main factors that influence how people make decisions?
- Introduce the POWER model to decision-making. This involves thinking through five sequential steps in order to make an effective decision: (1) define the problem—find out what causes it and why; (2) consider the options—find out

more than one way to solve the problem; (3) weigh the options—consider the consequences of each alternative, both for one's self and for others; (4) elect the best option; (5) reflect on the choice after it has been made—was it the best choice in hindsight?

- Is this a useful way to think about decision-making?
- Why might it be difficult to use this approach to making decisions?

(Kicking AIDS Out, 2001)

Along with conflict reduction/resolution skills, a culture of peace is more likely when the participants have also learned and practiced the other long-term social development skills in their development through sports programs. There is an obvious relationship between a culture of peace and the learning of skills designed to improve youths' ability to establish and maintain good relationships within an ever broadening environment in which a tolerance of and appreciation for diversity is encouraged. A culture of peace is also more likely when youth have high levels of communication skill, feel empowered, have high self-esteem, understand the importance of teamwork and goal setting, and are well-versed in making ethical decisions. As previously explained, a culture of peace is developed through sports; sports is about participation, inclusion and citizenship, and it unites individuals and communities by demonstrating commonalities and bridging cultural and ethnic divides. The very nature of sports provides the opportunity to learn social skills, such as discipline, confidence, and leadership, while also teaching important principles such as tolerance, cooperation, and respect. Sports teaches work ethic and how to manage victory and defeat (United Nations, 2003).

The acquisition of social development skills, including conflict reduction, is particularly important with the recent use of sports for development programs in post-disaster interventions (ICSSPE, 2009). When disasters have natural origins, such as earthquakes, tsunamis, floods, or hurricanes, emergency *development through sports* programs can provide a "return to normality" for affected youth. More than just a diversion, such programs can provide displaced youth with opportunities to learn and practice important social development skills under stressful conditions.

When a disaster is the result of ongoing (or past) man-made conflict, the teaching of conflict reduction skills through sports takes on major importance, and makes this cost-effective approach to life skills development an important initiative for internally displaced persons living in camps.

In the case of disadvantaged communities, where man-made conflict is the result of poverty and social marginalization, and thus the struggle for higher socioeconomic status, teaching social development skills, including self-esteem, through sports plays an important role in empowering the children and youth. *Development through sports* programs can provide disadvantaged youth with opportunities to learn and practice life-skills to improve their chances of further education and employment opportunities.

An example of *Development through sports* programs and how sports generates a culture of peace is one of CGC's programs in Africa, Leaders in Training (LIT), situated in Swaziland and led by the Sports and Olympic Council of Swaziland, which empowers youth by training them to become coaches and program leaders. The newly trained youth then run grassroots sports programs within their community and, as a result of their training in leadership, life-skills, HIV/AIDS education coaching, physical activity, and sexual health, act as mentors to the children in their community. LIT Manager comments on the positive impact of the program on participants and the community.

> *One of the volunteer leaders, who is now management for one of the LIT centres, noted the LIT training has helped her deal with issues that are of concern to herself and her community; issues she would have no way of addressing had she not taken that first step to becoming a volunteer. "Maybe we see there is a problem where there is someone who is abusing a child. We go to our community leaders and tell them about the kid and try to talk with the kid." Using a specific example, she added, "There is a kid here who is 11 years old and is getting abused by her uncle. He beats the child, the child is doing lots of bad things. We go to community leaders and we go to the home and now the matter is handled by police" (Interview, 2010).*

Another example of how sports is being used to foster positive social development is CGC's program in Lesotho, OlympAfrica Youth Ambassador Program (OYAP), led by the Lesotho National Olympic Committee, which empowers youth through sports to create positive change within their communities. One volunteer commented:

> *One participant witnessed firsthand what OYAP did for his own life, and now he wants to share that gift with other youth, whether they are volunteers or participants. "They gather skills on how to deal with their daily challenges. They*

gain confidence inside themselves and you can tell from a distance that this person is now able to answer for herself," he said, adding that participants are better able to resist negative peer influences from friends, and even family. "You can see a huge difference in the kids we have facilitated in our programs and the other kids who are not involved in our program." In particular, he noticed a significant improvement in girls who participate in the program, saying they appear much more self-confident and assertive than girls who haven't participated. He continued "Sport helps kids to keep engaged. When they are playing, they feel like they are part of the activity. And with our activities, we don't just dictate information to them, we introduce sport to them and after the sport, then you see what you have learned for yourselves, these activities make them aware of things they weren't able to do before. Sport makes them realize their talents" (Interview, 2010).

Conclusion

As such, throughout Africa and the Caribbean, CGC is working with partners to deliver *development through sports* programming. With the creation of the LTSDTS framework, CGC adapts existing programs and implements new programs to correspond sports and movement skills with social development skills appropriate for each age group through use of sports.

Sports can be, of course, an end in itself, providing a venue to engage in health enhancing physical activity, but it can also be more—much more, making a major contribution to the social development of disadvantaged youth and to a more peaceful world. This chapter has described a framework for the use of sports to achieve desirable social development objectives, including conflict reduction and therefore peace: a process known as *development through sports*. It is well placed to enhance the lives of disadvantaged children and young people since it can be implemented with a short planning and a few resources and can be tailored to their needs at each stage of their development.

We are at the early stages of using sports as a social intervention tool, and there is much to learn. CGC's LTSDTS framework is presented here in the spirit of Kaizen—the Japanese philosophy of continuous improvement. CGC would like to receive feedback on the ideas presented here and suggestions for improvement to the model, in particular, on what individuals and groups learn if and when they implement CGC's LTSDTS programs using this framework.

Questions for reflection

1. Are the seven stages of long-term social development through sports universal, or do they vary by region and/or culture?
2. Do the programs that exist in the Caribbean and Africa fit the CGC's LTSDTS framework, or do they need more specifications?
3. Are there other key areas of social learning besides the ones identified in the CGC's LTSDTS?
4. For intervention programs in disadvantaged communities, which stages of development should receive the most attention? Why?
5. How can sports organizations be influenced so that they become more focused on social development of youth than on high-performance results?

Notes

1 A play on the quote of Karl Von Clausewitz that "War is not an independent phenomenon, but the continuation of politics by different means."

2 Kicking AIDS Out (2001). Kicking AIDS Out was an initiative of the Edusport Foundation (a Zambian Sports NGO), which was adopted by NORAD (the Norwegian Development Agency) in 2001, in cooperation with the Norwegian Olympic and Paralympic Committee and Confederation of Sports (NIF). The Kicking AIDS Out initiative has grown to become an international network of organizations rallying around the power of sports to effect positive change in communities. The Kicking AIDS Out Network was established in Nairobi Kenya in 2001, where the first formal Network meeting took place, hosted by Mathare Youth Sports Association (MYSA). Kicking AIDS Out Network partners, associates, and members are from the United Kingdom, Canada, Kenya, Botswana, Namibia, Norway, South Africa, Tanzania, Swaziland, Lesotho, Zambia, Zimbabwe, Fiji, Papua New Guinea, Vietnam, and many countries in the Caribbean, including Guyana, Barbados, and Trinidad. The network shares information and best practices about the use of sports and physical activity in addressing HIV and AIDS, promotes policy development, shares resource materials, and supports local community-based projects. It provides a forum for exchange between organizations from different countries and continents—as equal partners—with different contributions. For more information, visit: *www.kickingaidsout.net*

3 The report was developed by Hannah Juneau, Colin Higgs, Rachael Kalaba, with additional material from Carla Thachuk.

4 Canadian Sport for Life (Long-Term Athlete Development) is a Canadian initiative to transform the design and delivery of participant-centerd sports programs. Details of the program, including all documentation, is available online at www.Canadiansportsforlife.ca.

Further reading

Canadian Sport Centre Pacific (CSC Pacific) (2005) Canadian Sport for Life: Long Term Athlete Development. Available at: www.canadiansportforlife.ca

Long-Term Athlete Development (LTAD) ensures that athletic programs are designed appropriately for the various developmental stages of individual atheletes.

The International Platform on Sport and Development. Available at: www.sportanddev.org.

The International Platform on Sport and Development website provides an information hub for the field of Sport and Development.

Sport for Development and Peace International Working Group. Available at: www.un.org.themes/sport.

The Sport for Development and Peace International Working Group (SDP IWG) is an inter-governmental body which provides policy advice to national governments regarding the integration of Sport for Development and Peace.

Generations for Peace. Available at: www.generationsforpeace.com.

Generations For Peace is a nonprofit organization dedicated to use sport for conflict transformation for purpose of sustainable peace building.

References

Canadian Sport Centre Pacific (CSC Pacific) (2005). *Long-Term Athlete Development: Canadian Sport for Life*. Available at: www.canadiansportforlife.ca.

Commonwealth Heads of Government (1991). *Harare Commowealth Declaration on Sport. Harare, Zimbabwe 20 October 1991.* Available at: *www.thecommonwealth.org/Templates/Internal.asp?NodeID=35773.*

Commonwealth Games Canada (1993). *The Commonwealth Sport Development Program.* Ottawa, Ontario: Commonwealth Games Association of Canada.

—(2009). *Report on Long-Term Social Development through Sport of the International Development Through Sport Unit.* Ottawa, Ontario: Commonwealth Games Canada.

Cooperative Republic of Guyana (2010). *A Sports Plan for the Cooperative Republic of Guyana.* Georgetown: Ministry of Culture, Youth and Sports.

Frawley, S., Veal, A. J., Cashman, R. and Toohey, K. (2009). *"Sport For All" and Major Sporting Events: Project Paper 1: Introduction to the Project.* School of Leisure, Sport and Tourism, University of Technology Sidney, Online Working Paper 6. Available at: *www.business.uts.edu.au/lst/research/publications/workingpapers/wp5frawley.pdf.*

Higgs, C. (2009). *CGC Review of programs in Swaziland, Lesotho, Botswana, and Namibia.* An internal report to Commonwealth Games Canada.

International Council for Sport Science and Physical Education (2009). Sport in Post Disaster Intervention. Available at: *http://www.icsspe.org/index.php?m=16&n=32&o=145.*

Kicking AIDS Out (2001). *Live Safe, Play Safe: Facilitator's Manual*. Nairobi: Kicking AIDS Out.

Peace and Sport (2010). *Corporate Brochure*. Available at: *http://www.peace-sport.org/images/pdf/PEACE_AND_SPORT_BROCH_UK.pdf*.

United Nations (1999). *Resolutions Adopted by the General Assembly*. General Assembly A/RES/53/243. New York: United Nations.

—(2003). *Sport for Development and Peace: Towards Achieving the Millennium Development Goals*. Report from the United Nations Inter-Agency Task Force on Sport for Development and Peace. New York: United Nations.

—(2010). Achieving the objectives of the United Nations through sport - Factsheet. Available at: *http://www.un.org/wcm/webdav/site/sport/shared/sport/pdfs/Backgrounders/NEW%20UNOSDP%20Backgrounder.pdf*.

Conclusions

Mitsuko Matsumoto

Chapter Outline

The book has explored where, why and how some groups of children and young people are disadvantaged in education and also how their disadvantage can be redressed. The book has done so by having seven case studies about education and groups of disadvantaged children and young people in different contexts. In this closing chapter, the insights offered by the studies are synthesized and some concluding thoughts are added.

Disadvantaged groups of children and young people

Given that this is only one volume, it is beyond its scope to map all the educationally disadvantaged groups of children and young people around the world. However, it is clear that different groups can be disadvantaged in different ways, both within and between countries. In India, Siddiqui identified the key disadvantaged groups as being girls, deprived urban children, children of migrant workers, children with special needs, children of Scheduled Castes

(SC), Scheduled Tribes (ST) and Muslims. Although some of these groups can be seen to be disadvantaged in other contexts, for example, deprived urban children in Ukraine and the United Kingdom, others are very context-specific; SCs and STs do not exist in other countries. In Vietnam, it is the poor rural locality that most needs an imaginative educational response, and one community in the Mekong delta has received it in the distinctive form of Goyer's NGO.

Factors that fuel educational disadvantage

As well as differences in the groups of children and young people that are disadvantaged depending on the context and history, the book has demonstrated that the factors that lead them to be disadvantaged in educational terms can be different. Disparities in the mainstream provision can itself be an issue. Schooling may not always be physically available, or may be out of reach economically. In most cases, a number of factors combine to produce multiple disadvantages. However, the economic factor, in the form of poverty, is probably the most pervasive, with gender discrimination often being combined with it in the form of the opportunity cost being higher in respect of sending girls to school. At least, that is often how it is perceived culturally. The poverty factor may kick in after primary school, as in the case described by Goyer, as well as before or during that initial phase, as shown by Siddiqui in India.

In some contexts, political factors play a large role in creating or perpetuating educational disadvantage. How the rights of formal education can be legally undermined for some groups of migrant children were demonstrated in the case of the United Kingdom, and for street children and orphan children, in the case of Ukraine. In Lebanon, Zakharia has shown that violent conflict and sequential political violence creates educational disadvantage in the sense that the pupils are psychologically affected by fear and trauma, as was also described in the introductory chapter in respect of Sierra Leone. A lack of political will to provide education for all children, combined with a weak government, can also be a factor.

Sociocultural factors also fuel educational disadvantage. In India, girls are often one of the educationally disadvantaged groups because there has not been a culture or social practice where girls are sent to school, and there are still many families that do not understand the value of sending girls to schools. Language can also be another factor. For some Scheduled Tribe children in India, whose mother tongue is not English, the fact that schooling is offered in English or a major local language, such as Hindi or Punjabi, creates additional barriers, even if the poor do have some access to schooling.

Psychological factors can be relevant, as indicated by Hantzopoulos and Goyer with regard to certain adolescents in New York and rural Vietnam respectively. Those adolescents in question did not feel that the higher level of schooling or the tertiary education is relevant to their lives or that they are competent to complete those levels of education. Consequently, the self-esteem required can be too weak to overcome the evident benefits of education. However, in those two very different cases and locations, they were able to show how imaginative interventions relevant to the locale can provide a successful humanitarian response in urban and rural settings alike.

From the discussion so far, the context, as well as individual factors, can be seen to contribute significantly to creating and perpetuating educational disadvantage. As Bourdieu has shown, education also tends to replicate and sustain situations of disparity, whether they be social, cultural, political or economic. Hantzopoulos contends that the top-down public school policy in the United States has only exacerbated existing educational inequalities, leading to the dropouts in already disadvantaged communities, their children and young people. O'Higgins and Evans, in turn, touch on how racism, discrimination and bullying against migrant young people and children are endemic in some schools and locations in the United Kingdom. Curricula perceived as irrelevant only go to strengthening the anomie of groups of adolescents in such contexts.

Potential educational responses to the disadvantage in education

Against the multi-layered and inter-related factors that fuel disadvantage in education as synthesized above, the writers in this volume have offered some potential responses that may begin to redress it. They are in the areas of pedagogy and curriculum, teachers and other role models, and policies.

Various pedagogical strategies and curricular innovations have been suggested by the case studies in the volume as potential ways to help the disadvantaged in education. Use of sports has been highlighted; *Coach for*

College in Vietnam employs team-based sports as a principal means to motivate rural deprived students to schooling and learning, as well as imparting academic knowledge through sports analogies. In turn, Chapter 7 shows how Commonwealth Games Canada utilizes sports in having the disadvantaged children and young people learn more about social issues, such as HIV/AIDS, and thereby make sports a direct means to promote health, development and a culture of peace.

It is not only with the use of sports that *Coach for College* attempts to help the rural middle school students in Vietnam. The central pedagogy of CFC is coined by Goyer as 'a learner-centered, constructivist pedagogy'. This means that the coaches, that is, Vietnamese and American college students, use an interactive teaching methodology, including asking of questions, small group work, role play, simulation and games. Goyer claims that this pedagogy helps students be excited about, and interested in, learning as well as allowing them to feel less inhibited.

Coach for College also focuses on teaching of life skills that are required as workforce in present day Vietnam. Such skills include productive beliefs about their ability and attributes, coping with failure if it happens, and developing the motivation and knowledge needed to develop long-term, academic-related life goals and self-regulation skills necessary for the achievement of goals.

The Shi`i school in Lebanon that Zakharia has adopted similarly uses an interactive and learner-centred pedagogy, but centring on community development as well as development of the learners themselves; she terms the school's approach 'a dynamic community empowerment model of schooling'. In terms of the personal development of learners, the school addresses it in an integrated manner, involving their social, emotional and cognitive needs. It targets the issue of direct violence (i.e., conflict and aftermath insecurity) and structural violence (e.g., gender relations and oppressive patterns of social, political and economic organization). It addresses these things not only through the formal curriculum, but also through extracurricular activities and special support structures, including counselling and scholarships.

The importance of teachers in making a difference in the schooling of educationally disadvantaged children and young people also comes out from the volume. This was most strongly argued by Hantzopoulos. She shows how teacher–student relationships can help pupils not only remain in school, but also attain higher achievement and raise aspirations for moving on to higher levels of education. From her analysis of pupils' voice, she identifies teachers as equals, a culture of trust, a culture of care, the concept of family and teachers as friends as important elements of student–teacher relationships that can help disadvantaged children and young people. In the Shi`i school that Zakharia has studied, too, the crucial role played by teachers to successfully manage the impact of direct and structural violence on pupils was apparent. It was they who guided the discussion to a constructive end, as demonstrated in the French writing lesson to overcome the negative feelings towards Israeli girls and in a book talk about political oppression. Sidiqqui also concludes his chapter with the importance of teachers. As well as the value of teachers engaging with the disadvantaged in schooling in a non-discriminatory manner, he emphasizes the importance of teachers' subject knowledge in providing disadvantaged children with a quality education. This is a neglected observation because in many of the circumstances of disadvantage, teachers are often only educated to a slightly higher level than the pupils. Many are unqualified. Nonetheless, by their attitudes and extracurricular care, they can still boost self-esteem and indicate ways for their students to overcome disadvantages to some degree.

In addition to teachers, older students can also help the disadvantaged in education. Goyer has shown how college students can serve as role models for rural, middle school students, motivating them to go into higher education. Vietnamese college students shared their stories about how they reached college as well as teach the classes as coaches, and these were important in making the rural students realize that it is possible to go into higher education and showed how this could be done.

Evidently, the chapters also suggest that laws or policies, at the national or local level, can help address the disadvantage in education and how they can best do so. Sidiqqui, in the case of India, and Danilko and Ivanenko, in the case of Ukraine, illustrated how government policies have improved the educational conditions of the various disadvantaged groups in their countries even though some of the policies and even regulations may sometimes be disregarded. This may be merely due to insufficient funding or appropriate staffing. For instance, the RTE Act 2009 in India ensured that children with disabilities are provided with free and compulsory education, and 66 per cent of them had been enrolled in some form of formal education by 2010. In the case of education for migrant children and young people in the United Kingdom, O'Higgins and Evans suggest that it may be best if local authorities provide universal support services within which specialist and targeted support for migrant young people is incorporated so that they would not be singled out by their status.

Concluding thoughts

Although it was not the intention or the scope of the volume to map out all the groups of disadvantaged children and young people and the issues that affect them, it has shown that different groups of children and young people are and can be disadvantaged, depending on the context and history. The book has also made it apparent that the notion that schools are, by nature, helpful to the disadvantaged is not always the case. Schools, through their tendency to reflect and replicate society, can perpetuate or even deepen the disadvantage experienced by some groups of children and young people. The quality of teachers is the key to overcoming this tendency, and quality is not just a matter of qualifications.

As argued in the introductory chapter, context matters. Although the book has shown some successful stories of schools or educational programmes, the same programme may not necessarily work in another context or with a different group of disadvantaged children. The importance of understanding who the disadvantaged children and young people are, as contextualized in the community and society in which they live, has been emphasized.

In many ways, this volume is just a first step in attempting to highlight, and respond to, educational disadvantage on a global scale, but in a range of specific contexts and to begin to address it. It is hoped that more studies on disadvantaged children and young people are undertaken and also that the volume inspires various innovative interventions to help disadvantaged children and young people in locations other than those represented here.

Index